This edition of

Robert Burns'
VALLEY OF DOON
An Ayrshire Journey Down Memory Lane
ISBN 0 9522720 2 4

Is limited to 1000 copies

By

Donald L Reid BA FSA Scot
Author of
Old Dalmellington Patna & Waterside
Doon Valley Memories
Doon Valley Bygones
Yesterday's Patna & The Lost Villages of Doon Valley
and other books

A ROYALTY FROM SALES OF THIS BOOK WILL BENEFIT
THE DALMELLINGTON BAND

Robert Burns'
VALLEY OF DOON
An Ayrshire Journey Down Memory Lane
ISBN 0 9522720 2 4
is dedicated to
A real gem with a heart of gold - my wife Kathleen

Published by
Donald L Reid
President
Beith & District Writers and Speakers Group
7 Manuel Avenue
Beith, North Ayrshire, Scotland KA15 1BJ
Tel: 01505-503801
E: donaldleesreid@hotmail.com
Web: http://donaldreid.mysite.wanadoo-members.co.uk
Web: http://henryfaulds.mysite.wanadoo-members.co.uk
Web: http://barrmilljollybeggars.mysite.wanadoo-members.co.uk
Web: http://ayrshirebooks.mysite.wanadoo-members.co.uk
.

2005

Design and production by
Delta•Mike•Golf
Printed in Great Britain by
Iain Crosbie Printers, BEITH, Scotland Tel: 01505-504848

Foreword by
Cathy Jamieson, MSP
Minister for Justice
The Scottish Executive

Poem
Standing on the Brig o' Doon
By
Rowena M Love

Craigengillan - A Vision of Stewardship
By
Mark Gibson

Waterside Revisited
By
Alice R Robertson

Childhood Memories of Lethanhill - A Ghost Village
By
Ann McLean (Donohoe)

All other material in the book researched and edited
by
Donald L Reid, 2005
First published in the United Kingdom, 2005
By Beith & District Writers and Speakers Group,
Enquiries regarding book sales to:
Donald L Reid,
7 Manuel Avenue, Beith, North Ayrshire, Scotland KA15 1BJ
Telephone: 01505-503801
E: donaldleesreid@hotmail.com

2005 Donald L Reid

The author is indebted once again to fellow Ayrshire author, Rowena M Love, for kindly agreeing to write a poem reflecting the spirit of *Robert Burns' Valley of Doon*. Great-granddaughter of an Ayrshire miner, Rowena is a writer and poet based in the West of Scotland. She is an experienced tutor and performer and is currently Writer in Residence for local charity, Writability. Her poetry collection, *The Chameleon of Happiness*, was published in March 2004 by Makar Press, a poetry collective she helped form. You can find out more about Rowena on her web site:
www.rowenamlove.co.uk

Standing on the Brig o' Doon
by
Rowena M Love

Sun-warmed stone beneath my hands,
water below; inspiration all around.
Close by, gardens erupt in colour,
Tam's Meg whinnies in the breeze;
my senses reel.

In mind's eye, I travel
to where Merrick's glacier gouged the land,
like Burns our hearts,
spreading granite wide to Wales;
his words, the world.

Still the Doon,
often grey as Mesolithic flints,
sparks memory of people past,
or sparkling in sunlight
bright as Loch Enoch sand,
sharpens history's blade:
cutting through time
as doggedly as it did Ness Glen.

Deep in the flow,
spectres of farmers, miners, bandsmen,
covenanters
spin swifter than Handsome Nell could dance,
while twigs toss – forestry splinters
or echoes of Pictish canoes?

Dandelion clocks drift in parody
of Blue Peter's parachute;
near the bank shadows flicker
their mimicry of Loch Doon's flicks –
gunnery ghosts unspool in the eddies;
lost villages sink.

Along the Doon's full length,
poetry pools coal-dark
or iridescent as dragonflies.

Robert Burns'
VALLEY OF DOON
An Ayrshire Journey Down Memory Lane

Foreword by
Cathy Jamieson, MSP
Minister for Justice
The Scottish Executive

Ye banks and braes o' bonnie Doon,
How can ye bloom sae fresh and fair?
How can ye chant, ye little birds,
And I sae weary fu' o' care?
Thou'll break my heart, thou warbling
bird,
That wantons thro' the flowering thorn:
Thou minds me o' departed joys,
Departed never to return

The Banks O' Doon
Robert Burns

It gives me great pride to have the honour of serving as the Member of the Scottish Parliament for a large part of East and South Ayrshire, which encompasses most of the area known and loved by many as the Doon Valley. In my regular travels about the constituency, meeting so many interesting local folk in an area which has towns, villages, lochs, moors and mountains, is simply an added bonus in this terrifically scenic valley of the River Doon. Local poets, authors and artists who fallen under its magical spell, have been inspired to capture the spirit of the Doon Valley. It is a spirit which can sometimes seem elusive in definition, but perhaps caring and sharing is central to it. This will strike a chord with older folk in particular who remember difficult days. As Robert Burns so eloquently put it in Epistle to Davie, A Brother Poet,

'We may be wise, or rich or great,
But never can be blest;
Nae treasurers nor pleasures
Could make us happy lang;
The hearts ay's the part ay,
That makes us right or wrang.'

The lingering joy of Donald L Reid's previous books on the Doon Valley is that they take the reader beneath this familiar surface, beyond what we can actually see and affectionately, layer by layer, uncover some of the events and influences which shaped the lively industrial past, the countryside and most importantly the indomitable spirit of ordinary people of the Doon Valley. I am sure that this book, like his others on the Doon Valley, will quickly become a prized possession by valley folk living both locally and firth of these shores. Donald L Reid has the ability to bring history vividly to life, and to make it relevant today, to young and old alike. Every community should have someone like Donald who works hard at capturing the past for the benefit of those who follow in our footsteps.

I have had the good fortune to travel fairly widely in my role as a Member of the Scottish Parliament and Scottish Executive and I have found one thing to be true. However brief a glimpse they may have had, people do not forget the Doon Valley with its grim history of iron production and coal mining that saw the

Cathy Jamieson, is Labour and Co-op MSP for Carrick, Cumnock & Doon Valley and Justice Minister in the Scottish Executive. She is also deputy leader of the Labour Group in the Scottish Parliament. Cathy takes a great interest in her constituency and has been a very energetic minister. She kindly contributed the foreword to this book.

development of communities which took a pride in working hard to raise families in what were often difficult circumstances. When I have spoken about the Doon Valley I have seen the name kindle a smile on the grimmest faces in the most remote of places. The towns and villages of the Doon Valley have certainly made their mark on folk all over the world and that is something of which we should all be very proud.

Donald L Reid is very proud of his Dalmellington roots. In this, his twelfth Ayrshire local history title and fifth specifically relating to the Doon Valley, he shares his unquenchable enthusiasm and knowledge he has gleaned from talking to many folk and carrying out much research.

I hope this richly informative and enjoyable book helps everyone who reads it derive more pleasure and interest from a visit and hopefully many return visits to the Doon Valley villages and its wonderful heritage museums at Dalmellington and Dunaskin. In so doing they will be able to better appreciate the unique social history, character and

beauty of the area by knowing something of what made it as it is today.

I asked Donald about his keen interest in the Doon Valley. He enthused, "I simply love it. I am staunchly proud of the folk who came before me and of a heritage of mining, both ironstone and coal, which produced proud independent down-to-earth folk with a sense of community spirit which I have rarely found anywhere else. In the Doon Valley and nearby Galloway Hills the scenery is stunning and there is always something new to learn if the time and trouble is taken to look. I simply hope that others will wish to remember the importance of and reflect upon the social history of this wonderful area where I spent my happy formative years."

Like Donald Reid, I am proud to be associated with the Doon Valley and its people. I hope his book makes you feel the same.

Cathy Jamieson

Aft hae I rov'd by bonie Doon,
To see the rose and woodbine twine;
And ilka bird sang o' its Luve,
And fondly sae did I o' mine;
Wi' lightsome heart I pu'd a rose,
Fu' sweet upon its thorny tree!
And my fause Luver staw my rose –
But ah! he left the thorn wi' me.

The Banks O' Doon
Robert Burns

CONTENTS

Festival of Sport held in Ayr in 1951 showing the team from Dalmellington who took part in a basketball tournament at Dam Park.
Back row (l to r): Robert Moffat, Robert Bell, John Semple, Hugh Gray, Jack Haynes.
Front row: Farquar McDougall, Tom Hutchison, Billy Giillespie and Jim Clark. Adult believed to be Sam Graham.

INTRODUCTION

The days of a bustling industrial past in the Doon Valley with iron and coal mining and brick making are now over. The Valley is now firmly in a post-industrial period, bringing new challenges and social change, but Doon Valley folk will, I hope, always be proud of their rich industrial heritage.

Remembering and recording factual information for those who follow in our footsteps is important. The fertile social history of any locality allows our young people the opportunity to better appreciate the social and political forces which brings them to their unique time and place in history. This book aims to help to do just that, at least in a small way.

This retrospective of the Doon Valley is the outcome resulting from many local folk of yesteryear buying cheap cameras and taking shots of people, places and events which we look at in awe and amazement. It is also an attempt to preserve a little more of the social history of the area. Most of the original photographers are unknown, but the fact that their photographs continue to give pleasure to the people of today would doubtless have given them great satisfaction.

And, of course, there has been so much to record by those astute enough to realise the speed of change and its social significance. When you look back over the past 70 years - a relatively short period of time - our country's history has produced such massive changes that they are all-too-easily taken for granted. These changes include sending man to the moon, mobile phones, jumbo jets, supersonic aircraft, microwaves, photo-copiers, ovens, washing machines, dishwashers, satellite television, compact discs and DVD, the common ownership of motor cars, credit cards, auto-banking, foreign holidays, supermarkets, 'superloos', house ownership by ordinary working people, heart and organ transplants and, of course, industrial change on a scale never previously contemplated by our forefathers with the decimation of the steelwork, fishing, shipbuilding and mining industries of Scotland. Conversely, another amazing change is the huge amounts of coal now won in East Ayrshire by opencast mining methods.

Some of the photographs take us back to the thirties (1930s). Older folk will tell you they were anything but 'good old days.' In the Doon Valley miners were unemployed and it was hard for ordinary folk to make ends meet. Tuberculosis and unemployment were the scourge of these and subsequent years. Enlightened treatment, hygiene, diet, improved housing and sanitation vanquished the 'White Death,' which was for long a mass killer. However, there was tremendous affinity amongst ordinary working families and neighbours in the Doon Valley, a feature of most mining communities. Everyone faced the same hardships and deprivation and there was a common bond of compassion and

But pleasures are like poppies spread,
You seize the flow'r, its bloom is shed;
Or like the snow falls in the river,
A moment white – then melts forever;
Or like the borealis race,
That flit ere you can point their place;
Or like the rainbow's lovely form
Evanishing amid the storm.

Tam O' Shanter
Robert Burns

The famous Bogton Mine aerial skylink ran between Bogton Mine and the coal washing plant at Minnivey Pit and stretched for just over 1 mile. A similar skylink ran from Minnivey to Chalmerston. This was later removed to the Butlins Holiday Camp at Heads of Ayr where it was re-erected and used to transport visitors from the camp entrance to the chalets below. Bogton mine was in the process of driving in 1930 and it closed in July 1954. There were four managers during that time, namely, Tom Hill, Hugh Anderson, James Lorimer and Tom Kerr. Approximately 80 miners worked at Bogton and they were transferred to Pennyvenie and Beoch in 1954.

We write our names upon the sands,
Like children in an hour of play,
And build the castles of our dreams
That vanish in the waves away.

The names engraven on the sands
Endure a circle of the clock;
But one man in a million carves
His name upon the solid rock.

Immortality
W D Cocker

understanding which took the practical form of helping each other through hard times and celebrating together in happier periods. Can anyone honestly say that there is the same spirit of caring in our communities today which was so evident in the mining villages of Doon Valley certainly up until the post-industrial era began in earnest with the closure of Pennyvenie Colliery in 1978.

Robert Burns wrote immortal verse around the rivers Ayr, Nith and Doon. In Dalmellington, Robert Hetrick (1769 – 1849), the blacksmith poet, was also busy penning lines which would help to immortalise the village and district. So, too, did another local word-smith, Matthew Anderson (1864 – 1948), the famous policeman-poet of the Ayrshire Constabulary, who was born at Waterside, a stone-throw away from the famous river. Indeed Burns and his local followers did much more than write poetry in praise of a river; they all helped to immortalise the Banks o' Doon so that anyone with even the most rudimentary knowledge of Scottish history, will instantly know of its most famous river. And of course it is arguable that the most strikingly scenic areas of the river are to be found in the upper reaches of the Doon Valley from Dalrymple to Loch Doon. Notably, when the river pours from that loch, the first tumbling mile is the greatest and most dramatic as it passes through the awe-inspiring Ness Glen made famous by Hetrick in his poem, Craigs of Ness.

Finally, it has to be acknowledged that this work is that of a keen amateur historian, motivated only by a genuine pride in his Doon Valley heritage and a desire to do something for the common good. It simply presents a limited picture, in words and photographs, of the district as it was yesterday and today. It makes absolutely no claim to be a definitive history, if indeed such was possible.

In concluding these remarks I should mention the wonderful response I received to my last book, Yesterday's Patna & The Lost Villages of Doon Valley. Copies winged their way to folk with Doon Valley roots in USA, Canada, Australia, New Zealand, South Africa and even to Khazakstan. It seemed to touch a chord of understanding, especially for those who lived in the Lost Villages. The many letters and phone calls of appreciation were greatly encouraging and spurred me on to produce the book you are currently reading.

One major aim in producing this book is to enable young folk in particular to learn about their unique social and industrial history. Another is simply to highlight the joys of the Doon Valley with its rich history, scenic beauty and friendly people to the prospective tourist or visitor.

I hope you enjoy what is the combined effort of many generous folk. Here, then, is Robert Burns' Valley of Doon.

Donald L Reid

ACKNOWLEDGEMENTS

Dalmellington and its environs have always been very special to the writer, hence the appropriateness of the little poem adjacent. I had the good fortune of being brought up in Bellsbank, Dalmellington where the friendliness of the folk and its special community spirit was a hallmark of village life. The building of Bellsbank Housing Scheme beginning around 1948 was a great boon to the area and afforded good housing for folk who moved from Benwhat and Corbie Craigs. Like my own parents, it also allowed many young couples with children to move from rented rooms to their first home. In the post war period most young couples had to live in 'digs', usually a rented room, until they were allocated a Council house.

I also had the good fortune to develop a love for the works of Robert Burns which grows stronger with each passing year. And of course from my earliest days I enjoyed walking in the upper reaches of the River Doon. Its breathtaking backcloth ranging from the dramatic cliffs of Ness Glen to the dominating hill ranges of Merrick, Mulwharchar and the Rhinns of Kells to the more gently sloping hills make this area very special to me and countless others. I never tire of visiting Loch Doon and this was a love affair that began from my earliest days picnicking by the loch on regular family outings with many friends of early days. The ever changing light and shade and the forest walk from my home in Bellsbank, made this area

simply magical in my boyhood days and it has seemed so to me ever since. The exquisite beauty of the Loch Doon and Galloway hills attracted me time and again. I have many happy memories of delightful sojourns to Loch Enoch, the Merrick, Back Hill o' Bush and White Laggan bothies in all weather conditions.

I should like to express my heartfelt thanks to everyone in the Doon Valley and further afield who gave me so much help during my research for this book. The success of its predecessors, *Old Dalmellington, Patna & Waterside, Doon Valley Memories, Doon Valley Bygones* and *Yesterday's Patna & The Lost Villages of Doon*, prompted me to once again put pen to paper. The previous books clearly touched many hearts, which was very gratifying. What always amazes me is the fact that folk with Doon Valley connections are to be found all over the world and they are very proud of their heritage. This wonderful response to my previous books gave me great personal satisfaction and encouragement to write this book recording more of the history of the valley of yesterday and today.

As we get older we all seem to enjoy looking back on those halcyon days of yesteryear and think of people, places and events, special in our lives. I hope this journey down memory lane will keep the memory fresh for you, and be for your children, and your children's children, a glimpse of a world they never

God gives all men all earth to love,
But, since man's heart is small,
Ordains for each one spot shall prove
Beloved over all

Rudyard Kipling

9

I count each day a little life,
With birth and death complete;
I cloister it from care and strife
And keep it sane and sweet.
With eager eyes I greet the morn,
Exultant as a boy,
Knowing that I am newly born
To wonder and to joy.
And when the sunset splendours wane
And ripe for rest am I,
Knowing that I will live again,
Exultantly I die.
O that all Life were but a Day
Sunny and sweet and sane!
And that at Even I might say:
"I sleep to wake again."

Each Day A Life
Robert W. Service

knew. A world which, with sorrows intermingled with the gladness of life, produced a race of men who were very proud, family men.

For most of us the upper valley of the River Doon will be remembered as a beautiful friendly area full of wonderful larger-than-life characters. I am immensely proud of my roots, my parents, my own family and the folk of yesterday and today in Dalmellington. I have also been intrigued by what appears to be an insatiable appetite for books and information on the Doon Valley. All five of my previous Doon Valley books sold out within a matter of months and copies winged their way to countries all over the world to interested readers with Doon Valley roots. My own personal philosophy is encapsulated in this verse from the pen of another popular poet, Robert W Service, which is simply to live life to the full every single day.

I am delighted and grateful that Cathy Jamieson, MSP, despite her busy ministerial commitments, agreed to write the foreword to this book. Special mention must go to Ayrshire poet, Rowena M Love, Alice R Robertson formerly of Waterside and Patna, now living in Edinburgh, Ann McLean of Kilmaurs and Mark Gibson of Craigengillan, Dalmellington for their individual contributions. I am sure they will touch a chord with readers. To Dot Graham for her helpful advice and guidance in relation to producing the manuscript and photographs into book form. Thank you Dot! A very special word of thanks to my wife, Kathleen Reid, daughter Elaine Reid, son Fraser Reid and his wife, Heather and grandson, Taylor James Reid for their unstinting support in all my writing projects. I am proud to say that I was richly blessed with the most wonderful family. A special word of thanks to my father, James Lees Reid and my late mother, Mary Hose Reid. To them I owe a great debt of gratitude for developing my interest in the byways of the Valley of Doon.

Special friends, Iain and Colette Shaw of Ardrossan, for their enthusiastic help dealing with photographs, captions, helpful suggestions and accompanying Kathleen and I on countless wonderful days out in Ayrshire and Galloway. Peter Barr of Kilmarnock, of whom in earlier days I recall with a smile many great cycling days mainly in the byways and hill tracks of Galloway, together with another great cycling pal and wonderful character, Bill Frew of Sorn. Peter Barr, a retired teacher, kindly read the manuscript and made many helpful suggestions as did Iain and Colette Shaw.

It would be remiss not to give a special mention to the editor and staff of the Ayrshire Post, Cumnock Chronicle and Ardrossan & Saltcoats Herald. They have all been tremendously supportive of all my Doon Valley books giving excellent reviews, which helped publicise my work to a wide readership in Ayrshire. Tony Collins of Bellsbank Men's Group; Hugh Johnstone MBE, the giant original man of Dalmellington for his usual kind and patient assistance and for a life-time of dedication to my good friends at the Dalmellington Band. His wife, Jenny, who unexpectedly died on 15 February 2003 was one of the many energetic unsung heroes who worked tirelessly over many years for Dalmellington Band. Jenny will be fondly remembered.

I am also grateful to the following individuals, mainly from Dalmellington. Ella Baird; Bill Bakkon formerly of Corbie Craigs and now living in Norway; Jim and Margaret Bowie; Stanley E Brodie QC, Jim Buchanan; Margaret B Davidson of Edinburgh and formerly of Lethanhill; William Coughtrie of Ayr via The Mill, Dalmellington; Ralph J Davidson who worked tirelessly to discover the remains of Spitfire Blue Peter on Cairnsmore of Carsphairn; John Dinwoodie; Robert (Rab) Douglas of Prestwick via Dalmellington; Louise Dunn (Scott) formerly of Waterside; Anne Geddes of the Baird Institute, Cumnock; Libby Gibson of Ayr Road Garage, Dalmellington for kindly

assisting with marketing this and previous books; John Grant of Ayr; Fransico Haro of Stewarton, Maureen Henderson of Ayr; my aunt Agnes Hose who always unstintingly thinks of others before herself; Giles Hutchison of Patna, Jan Hutchison, John Hutchison; Billy Johnstone of Patna; Anne Joss MBE, Alexander Kennedy, head teacher, Bellsbank Primary School; Jennifer King of Newcastle-upon-Tyne; Bobby and Margaret Knox of Patna; Mary Long of Ayr; Penny McCreath of Dalmellington; Janet McConnachie of Burnton; Patrick McCutcheon of Dalmellington for superb help with photographs and marketing this and other Doon Valley books; Minnie McNae of Polnessan; Miss Anna McHattie; Ian Muir of Monifieth, Angus; May Mullholland formerly of Polnessan now in Monifieth; Bert and Elizabeth Ritchie - Bert is the passionate president of Dalmellington Band. I was his best man and he was mine. It is generally

The last shift to work at Pennyvenie Colliery, Dalmellington, heralding the beginning the post industrial period in the Doon Valley. Closed July 1978.

Memory brings back to me
Starlit night and starlit sea,
While a boat at anchor lay
In a little land-locked bay

Never shall the night again
Hold the magic it did then;
Never shall so bright a moon
Shine upon a night in June

A Memory
W D Cocker

acknowledged that Bert and I ranked high in the table of worst trombone players in the whole world, albeit I was certainly top of the league; Madge Smith of Dalrymple; Stanley Sarsfield and Elaine Jones of Cathcartson Heritage Museum, Dalmellington; Forbes Taylor; Edward Uriarte (Sen) of Ayr; Tom and Alice Wallace; and Rev Kenneth Yorke of the linked charge of Dalmellington with Patna.

A special word of thanks is also due to Iain Crosbie, Printer, Beith and his excellent staff. Their work on my last book, *Yesterday's Patna and The Lost Villages of Doon Valley*, was widely acclaimed. I am delighted that this book has also been printed by a quality company in Beith, Ayrshire, where I now live.

I have continued to enjoy the unstinting hospitality of generous friends, David and Margaret Rarity of Patna who gave me unrestricted access to the late Scott J Rarity's Doon Valley photographic collection and I hope to publish more Doon Valley photographic books in future, the next book being *Ayrshire's Doon Valley - Through the Lense* in May 2006. They have also gained much pleasure from weekly visits from my wonderful grandson, Taylor James Reid (18 months), who has brought them great joy, too.

In compiling a list of acknowledgements there is always a very real fear that someone who has given important assistance will be missed out. I sincerely hope that has not happened, but in case it

has I can only beg forgiveness, express appreciation and lay the blame on a faulty memory which is definitely not improving with age! The photographs in the book have come from a variety of different sources and with the passage of time the original sources are unknown. If the copyright of anyone has been infringed, I apologise profusely in advance for unintentional error. I should also say that endeavouring to identify everyone in the many photographs I have collected has been an enormously difficult and very time-consuming task. The minute a photograph is published someone immediately knows the names of those recorded with a question mark and utter those annoying words: 'You should have asked me!' So, to those who are shown in photographs as 'question marks' I beg forgiveness.

I have enjoyed researching and compiling this book which flows from a deep love the Doon Valley. I hope it will give you as much pleasure reading it and in doing so awaken long forgotten memories of yesteryear. Enjoy *Robert Burns' Valley of Doon*.

Donald L Reid

CHAPTER 1

OUR NATIONAL BARD

The life of Robert Burns is fascinating and has employed the pen of so many biographers, that it is often assumed that little remains which is new. However, with every new edition of the Burns Chronicle, it is amazing just how much interestingly different information about the poet and his life and times is unearthed by keen Burnsians. A report in the Scotsman (May 21, 2005) suggested that Robert Burns is contributing £3 million a week to the Scottish economy more than 200 years after his death mainly through visitors to places in Ayrshire and Dumfriesshire associated with the poet. Experts have calculated his brand value at £157 million a year with potential for growth.

The World Federation of Burns Clubs, with its headquarters in Kilmarnock, brings together admirers of the Bard from all corners of the globe, united in their appreciation of the works of Robert Burns. Every year thousands of visitors make that pilgrimage to the Auld Clay Biggin at Alloway and to many other places in Ayrshire, which lay claim to ownership of part of the spirit of the poet. That they continue to come year and after year is a phenomenon which places Robert Burns and his works head and shoulders above other poets and artists. There is an almost insatiable demand for more and more information about this great and very complex Scot who only lived for 37 short but very full years.

Even before the Burns Federation was formed in 1885 there were many Burns Clubs at home and overseas, instituted primarily to celebrate the anniversary of the birth of Robert Burns on 25 January and keep his memory green.

Since the beginning of the nineteenth century these celebrations have gone on increasing every year in number and exuberance. Ayrshire can lay claim to having many clubs, organisations and groups who hold an annual celebration and this is replicated right across the globe. Indeed the total number of Burns Suppers organised by Burns Clubs is reckoned to be less than five percent of the total celebrations held by all kinds of societies, clubs and organisations all over the world. At every Burns Supper there will be speeches, songs and poems. This mighty chorus of praise and adulation of a man is remarkable from every point of view. That it should resound in honour of a poet is perhaps the most remarkable thing about it.

Why, then, do we honour Burns today? What is so unusual about his character and background that he should be treated in such a peculiarly special manner. There is no benchmark to measure him against others because he is treated in a way not afforded to any of our great writers, politicians, churchmen, scientists, explorers, footballers, athletes or even monarchs. It is, of course, easy to poke fun at the cult of the Burns Supper. Hugh MacDiarmid in *A Drunk*

Should auld acquaintance be forgot,
And never brought to mind?
Should auld acquaintance be forgot,
And days o' lang syne?

Robert Burns

Man Looks At The Thistle, writes disparagingly and somewhat arrogantly:

"No' wan in fifty kens a wurd Burns wrote
But misapplied is a'budy's property,
And gin there was his like alive the day
They'd be the last a kennin' haund to gi'e

Croose London Scotties, wi' their braw shirt fronts
And a' their fancy freen's, rejoicin'
That similar gatherings in Timbuctoo,
Bagdad – and Hell, nae doot – are voicin'

Burns' sentiments o' universal love,
In pidgin English or in wild-fowl Scots,
And toastin' ane wha's nocht to them but an
Excuse for faitherin' Genius wi' their thouchts.

No one can pretend that all those who congregate at such celebrations are models of wisdom and decorum. Indeed if they were it might just be a very dull gathering lacking in charm and real character. That would be equally true of any other function where people come together for a social occasion. Burns clubs are very proud of their traditions in honouring the bard. However, even the great MacDiarmid is perhaps guilty of high-handedness in denying the ordinary Scot the right to make comment on what makes Robert Burns special. Our poet is after all, all things to all men, and has this world-wide acclaim which is unique. That is what makes him such an interesting character and few lives have been dissected and laid open to critical examination like that of Robert Burns.

Having a degree or being academic is certainly not required to appreciate the works of Burns. All that is needed is open a book of his poems and read them and they will often touch the heart. Joining a Burns Club will deepen personal appreciation with other like-minded enthusiasts sharing their views on the bard and his works. Countless readers will have enjoyed attending memorable Burns and St Andrew's celebrations where ordinary men and women provided the most fascinating and remarkable knowledge and insights into the life and works of the poet and all things Scottish.

For that is the mark of the Scot of all classes: that he stands in
An attitude towards the past unthinkable to Englishmen, and
Remembers and cherishes the memory of his forebears, good
Or bad; and there burns alive in him a sense of identity with
The dead even to the twentieth generation

Weir of Hermiston (1896, Ch. 5)
Robert Louis Stevenson

Burns Suppers do have a worthy element in them. The speakers, readers and singers brave enough to stand up and attempt to entertain and educate their fellows are surely to be commended as they help to keep alive a tradition which although currently strong, should never be taken for granted. Many would agree with the view that some of the best toasts to the immortal memory were delivered by ordinary folk in kirk halls, bowling clubs and community centres. The term ordinary folk should not be regarded as a pejorative term. Rather it is always inspirational when an ordinary person, without any great educational background, but steeped in Burns-lore, is able to express a genuine and intimate love for the works of the bard in tribute, poem and song to the delight of his fellows. Long may that continue to be the backbone of the world-wide Burns movement.

The social, friendly, honest man,
Whate'er he be
This he fulfils great Nature's plan
And none by he.

Second Epistle To J Lapraik
Robert Burns

That any man could have achieved what Burns did in 37 short and difficult years, simply takes the breath away. Up till 1783 Burns had composed only about thirty pieces, few of any special merit. The following year brought a dozen more. However, in 1785 he produced more than forty poems, most of them longer and much more ambitious than anything previously attempted. His output was prolific and he now bore all the hallmarks of a truly gifted poet, that period producing all his most famous poems. Hans Hecht, one of the great biographers of Burns, wrote: "The floodtide of Burns's genius burst its bounds and began to sweep irresistibly forward." The young Ayrshire bard was on course to make his mark in a way never equalled in his time, our time or indeed perhaps not even in the future.

We only have to reflect on our own achievements in 37 years and the true genius of Robert Burns will become self-evident. But chiefly we honour him because he has given perfect expression to the common, everyday experiences of Scottish life in his time. He is pre-eminently the poet of the ordinary man. 'Auld Lang Syne' is as much an international anthem as 'A Man's A Man.' Whenever that song is sung those present are conscious of all the generations of mankind brought there by the genius of Robert Burns. In honouring him we pay homage to the best features of our frail humanity - friendship, tolerance, brotherhood and sympathy for all poor mortals gone astray.

Robert Burns made the Doon Valley famous when he immortalised it in The Banks O' Doon. From charming Loch Doon to the sea at Doonfoot, in a straight line, the River Doon runs generally north westerly, the distance is sixteen miles, but by the rivers winding course it is some twenty-six miles. In that distance it descends 700 ft running through some of the most dramatic and beautiful countryside to be found anywhere in Scotland. Burns mentions it many times, notably in Tam o' Shanter, and of course in the famous song immortalising the Doon Valley, The Banks O' Doon. This is arguably the most popular of all of Burns' songs and first appeared in the Scots Musical Museum in 1792. It also appeared in Thomson's Scottish Airs. In November 1794 in a letter to Thomson,

Burns asks: 'Do you know the history of the air? It is curious enough. A good man years ago, a Mr James Miller, Writer in your good town, a gentleman whom, possibly, you know - was in company with our friend Clarke, partly by way of a joke, told him to keep to the black keys of the harpsichord, and preserve some kind of rhythm.'

The River Doon certainly inspired Robert Burns and he in turn spurred many other local pensmen to verse from his day to our day. As we travel along the A713 from Ayr to the heart of the Doon Valley in Dalmellington we pass Waterside, also known as Dunaskin, with two chimneys still dominating the scene and standing sentinel over this unique industrial site. It was the arrival in 1845 of the Houldsworth family that significantly changed the social and industrial fabric of the Doon Valley and saw ironstone, coal and pig iron dominate the local economy for the following 140 years. However, the beginning of the end can be identified with the last tipping of slag from the blast furnaces at Waterside in 1921, thus marking an end to the production of pig iron. The closure of Pennyvenie Colliery in 1978 was also a significant date, marking the arrival of the post-industrial era in the Doon Valley.

Waterside or Dunaskin was a vibrant village and home to Matthew Anderson (1846 – 1948), a great admirer of the bard who in turn became known as the policeman-poet of the Ayrshire Constabulary. In Dalmellington, another wordsmith in the form of local blacksmith, Robert Hetrick (1769 –

1849) also had his poetic bent aroused by Scotia's bard. A collection of his poems was published in 1834. Two of his notebooks, containing verse interspersed with blacksmith's sketches and accounts, can be seen in the Cathcartson Museum and Visitor Centre, Dalmellington. Hetrick and Anderson were both to write poems that would encourage others to visit and appreciate the magical Valley of Doon.

Although the poetic output of these poets cannot be considered to be high art, they do something very important in terms of providing us with a flavour of their time in history. Anderson, in his role as a police officer, served for 38 years throughout Ayrshire and wrote many poems based on local occurrences and in tribute to those who impressed him. Conversely, Hetrick a weaver and blacksmith, was very proud of his Dalmellington roots and had a vision of a prosperous small town with a vibrant industrial base. In the following lines he refers to the principal heritor and to the dying weaving trade of the town:

His is the land of coals and metals,
For making coppers, pipes and kettles.
But if the public mind would settle
As I would hae't,
He could employ a thousand shuttles
On his estate.

Ironically, Hetrick died in 1849 just as a dramatic improvement in the Valley's fortunes was under way with the building of the Dalmellington Iron Works at Dunaskin and the opening of many coal and ironstone mines in what amounted to a mini-industrial revolution. Both are clearly steeped in the idiom of Burns and there is also great solidarity with the poor and downtrodden in society. They also describe local scenes and events which prove interesting to those who enjoy researching local history.

Hence, our National Bard can lay claim to inspiring other word-smiths to reflect on the social and economic happenings of their life and times in the Doon Valley. Even today our world-renowned poet continues to inspire others. In keeping with the spirit of the occasion, the historic official state opening ceremony of the Scottish Parliament on 1 July 1999 incorporated both traditional and modern themes in terms of prose and poetry. The programme included a Robert Burns song and a contemporary poem by the late Iain Crichton Smith, as well as a reading on the theme of Scotland by a national schools Burns competition winner.

Immediately after the Queen officially opened the parliament, well-known Scottish broadcaster Tom Fleming stood to recite The Beginning of a New Song, a previously unpublished poem by Iain Crichton Smith which calls for Scotland to "sing in a new world".

Let our three-voiced country
sing in a new world
joining the other rivers without dogma,
but with friendliness to all around her.
Let her new river shine on a day
that is fresh and glittering and
contemporary;
Let it be true to itself and to its origins

inventive, original, philosophical,
its institutions mirror its beauty;
then without shame we can esteem
ourselves.

The influence of Burns came to the fore with folk singer Sheena Wellington as she sang so movingly A Man's a Man for A' That from a balcony overlooking the hall before First Minister Donald Dewar thanked The Queen for the gift of the Mace, the symbol of the Parliament's authority. Those who watched this historic event on television will long remember that wonderful rendition by one of Scotland's truly gifted singers.

Robert Burns continues to touch the heart of each new generation as no other poet can. No doubt, he ran about his native braes, paddled in the burn, and gathered daisies like other children of his day. And of course Robert Burns was responsible for that great anthem that is sung at gatherings all over the world - the international anthem of friendship, Auld Lang Syne. The secret of this song is that it gives voice to the endearing sentiments of the human heart – love of home, parents and family; love of childhood days; and love of our friends. Only Robert Burns could do that.

We twa hae run about the braes,
And pu'd the gowans fine;
But we've wandered mony a weary foot
Sin' auld lang syne.

We twa hae paidled i' the burn,
From morning sun till dine;
But seas between us braid hae roar'd
Sin' auld lang syne.

In the final analysis, it is the humility of Burns, his kind heartedness, his proud independence, his strong democratic feeling, and his abiding faith in his Maker, and his human failing that endear him to his countrymen. For those who have associations with the Valley of Doon, no song is more striking than The Banks O' Doon which has brought fame to this fascinating corner of Ayrshire. If we walk along the Banks of Doon as they pass through Ness Glen and into calmer waters through Craigengillan and, in our mind's eye, we might just happen upon Rab the Rhymer.

Wi lightsome heart I pu'd a rose,
Fu' sweet upon its thorny tree;
And my fause luver stole my rose,
But, ah! He left the thorn wi' me.

The Banks o' Doon
Robert Burns

CHAPTER 2

RIVER DOON – SOURCE TO LOCH DOON

Geological studies reveal that it was some 450 million years ago when the Loch Doon hills were created. The Galloway hill group to the south of Loch Doon, was then being formed by the molten granite, dramatically erupting up through the sandstone rocks of the land. The hot liquid granite baked the surrounding rocks to form a ring of hills, a ring we now call the Rhinns of Kells and the Merrick, Galloway's highest hill. But it was between fourteen thousand and two million years ago that Loch Doon was formed. As the climate gradually grew colder, an ice cap developed on top of Merrick. This ice cap swelled over the land around it. The monstrous glacier gouged out the rock beneath it and carried massive boulders far away. For how else could boulders of Loch Doon granite have been found as far away as North Wales and Northern Ireland? What you see now, the forests, the plants, the remains of homes where people once lived, even the valley itself, is less than a blink of an eye in the life of this land. One can only speculate, in fourteen thousand years from now, how this beautiful land will have changed, but much depends on the way the people of today treat our environment.

Several hundred years ago the area around Loch Doon was not as deserted as it now seems. For instance, a few minutes walk from Loch Doon dam on the high ground just to the west, there is a place called Macnabstone, once a thriving farmstead. Archeologists speculate that this was once the home of a large family living close to the shores of the loch and they would have lived an almost entirely self-sufficient lifestyle. Traces can still be seen today of their rectangular stone house, their byre and outbuilding. If you think that no one could ever have grown crops like wheat and rye, barley and oats on the wild moors above this ancient loch, then why did they have a kiln?

But these hardy folk were not the first to settle on the shores of Loch Doon. Not by at least 8,000 years! The earliest inhabitants of Loch Doon were small groups of Mesolithic hunter-gatherers, who lived off the rich wild resources, the plants, fish and animals, of the valley around them. All they left behind as evidence of their presence were the flint blades, scrapers and arrow points that have been found by the loch over the years. Today the land around the loch is suitable only for forestry and rough grazing, but the tourists who flock to Loch Doon would be wise to remember that it was not always so and the fragile ecology of the area has to be guarded jealously to preserve it for future generations.

Loch Doon is an area of Special Scientific Interest (SSI) which makes it special in terms of flora and fauna and its overall natural resources. Little known to all but local fishermen and what makes this loch particularly special, is the cold silent world below the surface. This is

As down the burn they took their way,
And thro' the flowery dale;
His cheek to hers he aft did lay,
And love was ay the tale,
With "Mary, when shall we return,
Sic pleasure to renew?"
Quoth Mary "Love I like the burn,
And ay shall follow you."

As Down The Burn
Robert Burns

The majestic Merrick, highest hill in the south of Scotland taken from Loch Muck on the Ayrshire/Stewartry border.

the only location in southern Scotland where we find the elusive Arctic Char which occurs naturally sharing the loch with Brown Trout and Atlantic Salmon that spawn in the shallow gravel beds on the waters edge. Loch Doon is also home to a wide range of bird and plant life. The incessant trilling and fluty songs that can be heard along the length of the loch

The Wallace girls of Dalmellington on a camping holiday at Loch Doon around 1956
Left to right: Jean Wallace (McFadyean), Catherine Wallace (Mathieson), Marion Wallace (Thomson) and Mora Wallace (Jamieson).

belongs to skylarks. Listen out also for the distinctive and haunting 'coor-lee' of the Curlew, which abound in the hinterland of the loch on the wild moorland leading from Doon to Girvan Valleys. There is something haunting and

memorable about the call of the curlew.

Looking carefully the visitor may catch a glimpse of the common Sandpiper, mainly between April and August, as they fly in groups a few feet above the surface of the loch. Circling high above the southern end of the loch are Buzzards, so common now throughout Southern Scotland. A few miles further south is the stronghold of the Peregrine Falcon and the elusive Red Kites, recently re-introduced into Galloway from Wales. Deer are plentiful and entering the Galloway hills, expect to encounter wild goats, the mountain fox or perhaps also the less common Golden Eagle.

Recent regular sightings of playful otters near to Craigmalloch at the southern end of the loch, indicates that wildlife is managing to survive, perhaps perilously so, in tandem with an ever increasingly pernicious human presence on the loch in the form of semi-permanent encampments by caravaners on the banks of the loch, in excess of 100 being common in recent years. Many see this as a real danger to the fragile ecological balance of Loch Doon, an issue that has been largely ignored by the authorities.

By the shore of the loch and beside pools lurk killers that entice, trap and slowly digest their victims. Sinister indeed! But don't be scared because the Sundew plants only kill insects. All around the area you will find Bogmyrtle with its distinctive smell. Once used to flavour beer, experiments are ongoing to see if Bogmyrtle holds the secret of keeping the lochs people-eating midges at bay.

Overflow Loch Doon Dam

All around the loch you will find the hillsides covered in heather that provides honey still valued for its taste and apparent therapeutic properties.
The River Doon begins its journey to the Firth of Clyde at the foot of the mighty Merrick Hill in the remote area by Loch Enoch. This is an inspiring area to the keen hill-walker with its unsurpassed beauty and loneliness as it begins a journey of some 26 miles reaching the sea at Doonfoot near Ayr. On route it passes through the remote reaches of some of the finest uplands in Scotland with the grey Galloway Hills hosting this mighty river in its very earliest stages as it journeys through wild and lonely country. This is a land inhabited by deer, goat, fox, peregrine falcon, buzzard and golden eagle.

Walkers will find an almost never-ending number of conifer trees of different varieties, planted over hundreds of acres as a long term cash crop. These

Dalmellington folk having a short camping holiday near Loch Doon castle.
Back row (l to r): William 'Wull' Currie, David Wallace, Hugh Bunyan, Bill Wallace and Sam Semple. Man kneeling with crook, Willie Taylor.
Front row: Quintin Wallace others unknown.

fast growing trees, which can typically be harvested in 40 - 60 years, may be beneficial to the economy of Scotland, but certainly detract from this desolate land of mist, mountain and moor. They also create an almost continuous and very frustrating barrier to those who wish to explore the area today. However, on a fine day the scenery is outstanding from the higher ground above the tree-line. Some would even say spellbinding. Loch Enoch, lying at a height of 1,617 feet above sea-level, is one of the highest lochs in Scotland and in harsh winters is often partially ice-covered or ice-fringed.

This lonely loch is surrounded by the Merrick and Rig of Munshalloch to the west, the conical Mullwharchar (known in earlier times as The Star) to the north, the mighty Dungeon hill to the east and Craig Neldricken to the south. Until the post-Great War boom in outdoor activity in the late 1920s, this loch was visited by small numbers of enthusiastic walkers. However, with nearby Backhill o' Bush and White Laggan bothies providing overnight shelter for walkers, loch Enoch is now easily accessible to the many folk who enjoy exploring these lonely hills. Although the hills are relatively remote, an incredible plan was hatched in the early 1970s to bore some 32 tunnels into Mullwharchar which was to become a dustbin for nuclear waste. Public disquiet and protests soon persuaded the government of the momentous folly of this plan. It was then quietly dropped and hopefully will never be resurrected. However, locals and environmentalists should be ever vigilant. A report in the Cumnock Chronicle in 2005 ominously suggested that the plans for dumping nuclear waste at Mullwharchar were once again being revisited by Government faced with the problem of how to dispose of nuclear waste.

Dalmellington Badminton Club on their annual hike which normally involved them in walking to the Merrick via Glentrool. They are photographed by Bruce's Stone at Glentrool around 1948.
Back row: Jean Johnstone (Purdie), Alex Wallace
Second back row: Donald Tyson, Esther Wilson (Pringle), Jean McLarty (Horne)
Front row: Robert Wallace and Bert McClue.

The shores and sweeping bays of Loch Enoch contain beautiful white granite sand which shimmers in the sun, giving

A walk up Craiglee Hill above Loch Doon Castle in early 1950s.
Back row: Jim Wallace of Dalmellington
Middle row: Quinten Wallace, Tom Wallace and Bobby Wallace (stick)
Front (lower height): George Taylor and John Wallace.

the area a beauty all of its own. The area is also littered with rock debris and evidence of glaciation is abundant with many corries, moraines and erratic boulders in the area.

Indeed it can be said that the dramatic nature of the scenery is rather different from the rest of the Southern Uplands and is more akin to the wildest parts of the highlands. Perhaps this is why this most remote area of Galloway is so attractive to the committed hill walker, geologist and geographer. Even in midsummer, the water on Loch Enoch is crystal clear and biting cold. There are three islands located on the loch and on the largest there is an interesting feature known as 'loch-in-loch' which is effectively a small loch on this island. Loch Enoch is 127 feet deep and this was recorded by James McBain, author of the classic work *The Merrick and Neighbouring Hills*, who plumbed the depth during one particularly severe winter. He also wrote of this loch's trout having deformed fins, speculating that this was due to the underside of the fish rubbing on the granite basin of the loch. To the knowledge of the writer no such fish have ever been caught in Loch Enoch and it is likely that deformed trout, whilst being an interesting theory, is more likely to be part of folk-lore

From the 18th right through to the early 20th century the silver sand on the shores of Loch Enoch was used in a fascinating way by Galloway gypsies, packmen, sand vendors and later by farm labourers. They would visit this most remote of lochs, bag the silver sand and carry their extremely heavy and unwieldy loads to sell round the farms and clachans of Galloway. This trade is believed to be centuries old and the famous Loch Enoch sand was put to good use sharpening a variety of cutting tools. Although granite sand was also obtained from other Galloway lochs for this purpose, the most treasured of all came from wild Loch Enoch and a bag of sand represented many hours of demanding toil.

One of the last known sand vendors was Johnnie Morgan. He travelled the south-west in a cart that was pulled by Tommy, his donkey and sold sand, keel for hearthstones and doorsteps and straiks for applying the sand. It is reported that he died at the age of 85 in Thornhill Poorhouse, in 1901. After the Great War

the sharpening of tools with sand had largely been overtaken by sharpening stones. All but a few farmers and shepherds continued to use the famous silver sand of Loch Enoch until around the 1930s. S R Crockett, the Galloway author, created the character "Silver Sand" in his book, *The Raiders*, set in the Galloway hills. He describes (page 207) the qualities of Loch Enoch sand. *"But this,"* he said, taking up a smaller bag, as if it had been fine gold, *"is the silver sand of Loch Enoch itself. It is the best, the keenest and lies closest to the blade of the scythe."* S R Crockett, with his compelling novels set in Galloway's Raiderland, would today have been regarded as a Travel Agent's dream, bringing tourists to what was hitherto an unexplored but truly majestic corner of Scotland.

The Eglin Lane runs north from Loch Enoch and is joined by the Cauldron and Saugh Burns and other minor streams. After joining the Carrick Lane it eventually enters Loch Doon at its southern extremity. Thirteen lochs empty their excess water into Loch Doon. These are the Dry Loch draining into the Gala Lane, Loch Enoch, Twatchtan, Macaterick, Fanny, Slochy, Recawr, Goosie, Gower and Ballochling draining into the Whitespout Lane. Lochs Derclach and Finlas draining into the Garple Burn and Loch Muck, strangest of all, draining into Loch Doon from the east by way of underground channels. There are no obvious outlets from this loch, but into Loch Doon it must surely shed its excess waters.

The name Doon comes from the Gaelic *Duin,* which can mean either a hill or a fort. The Celts, when they came to Britain, made their bases on the high moors and ridges, and fortified the hilltops, so the word *Duin*, originally a hill, acquired a secondary meaning of fort. So, Loch Doon can be either "the loch of the hill ridges" or "the loch of the fortress." It is likely that the name is far older than any fortifications in the district and the river took its name from the Loch. But it is the once proud castle, which now sits on the west bank of the loch, which draws people back time and again.

But now my walls in ruin lie;
My rooms are mouldering to the sky;
Where lonely herons and houlets cry
Their cauldrife sang,
Unmix'd with harmony or joy,
The hale night lang.

Petition of Loch Doon Castle
Robert Hetrick

Loch Doon Castle, once known as Balloch Castle, is of ancient lineage and MacArthur states that the Galloway Picts used Castle Island to fight off invasion by the Cambrian Celts in the fourth century. The castle now stands proudly on the south west corner of the loch and is a popular visitor attraction. It is a splendid eleven sided curtain-walled castle designed to defend its original position on the southern end of Loch Doon on a site which can still be seen today towards the centre of the loch on castle island. The stonework is outstanding as evidenced by the

Tom Wallace (left) and Hugh Hainey of Dalmellington on a walk to Loch Neldricken where they stop for a rest in late 1950s or early 1960s. Hugh was the waterman in Dalmellington for many years.

beautifully hewn large blocks of ashlar, which have stood the test of time.

It is believed that the original castle was built after 1275 on a small island at the south end of the loch and most writers agree that it probably dates from the late 13th or early 14th century. However, it has been suggested by several historians that a much earlier settlement was also sited here. In 1306 and 1319 the castle was besieged by the English who periodically invaded southern Scotland for some time after Bannockburn in 1314. However, the castle remained impregnable as the depth of the surrounding water made it impossible for besiegers to build a causeway out to the castle. Furthermore, it was far enough from the land to make impotent most siege implements used for hurling large stones such as trebuchets and siege mangonels. The only effective way to defeat the castle was for the besiegers to remain in situ long enough to literally starve the garrison or take the castle by trickery or by negotiation.

Legend tells how Loch Doon Castle gave shelter and refuge to Robert the Bruce, hero King of Scotland, who fought some of his battles in the neighbourhood, notably the Battle of Glentrool, a few miles across the Galloway Hills from Loch Doon in 1307. Dargie suggests that this ancient seat of the Lords of Carrick, Loch Doon Castle first appears in documented history in the wake of Robert the Bruce's defeat at Methven in 1306. After helping the unseated Bruce back to his steed, Sir Christopher Seton and the remnants of his men quit the field at Methven and made for what he supposed was the safety of Loch Doon. Only a few days before he had a central place in the entourage of Scotland's new King. Now separated from his friends in what was then an inhospitable country, he was sure that Loch Doon Castle would provide safety and security. Having made a very narrow escape in evading the enemy it can only be imagined his relief at reaching Loch Doon, only for his dreams of rest and safety to be shattered. One can only begin to imagine Seton's despair when the castle governor, Gilbert De Carrick, believing that the House of Bruce had been totally vanquished, handed Sir Christopher over to the English force, hot on his trail. King Edward's vengeance was terrible. Seton was taken to Dumfries where he was subsequently hanged, drawn and quartered as a traitor - the same fate which befell William Wallace for daring to oppose English rule in Scotland

In 1333 Loch Doon was to earn a special place in the history of Scotland at what was then one of the lowest points in the Wars for Scottish Independence. Balloch Castle remained loyal to the Stewart cause and proudly flew the standard of David II when almost every other castle and stronghold in the land had decided to support the English puppet Edward Balliol. Only five others, Dumbarton, Urquhart, Lochmaben, Lochleven and Kildrummy, remained true to the patriot cause.

1446 was yet another famous time in the history of the castle. William, 8th Earl of Douglas, was keen to capture the castle as part of his ongoing feud with the neighbouring Kennedy Clan in the Girvan valley. This strategic stronghold survived the attack for several weeks, but its small garrison was no match for the might of the Douglas military machine and the castle was surrendered.

The castle seems to have seen many difficult times and doubtless the proud walls could tell many a fascinating tale. In the reign of King James V (1513 - 1542), who tried to curb the power of the Scottish Barons, the castle was burned down in the 1520s and the immense roof was thrown into the loch together with the iron portcullis where it is said it still remains to this day.

In 1823 nine ancient Pictish canoes, of hollowed oak 23 feet long, 2 foot 6 inches deep and 3 ft. 9 inches broad were discovered in the loch, pointing to a fascinating presence beside the loch in Pictish times. Three of the canoes were recovered, and one was sent to the Hunterian Museum in Glasgow, while the other two were placed in shallow water at the foot of the loch.

In the mid 1930s the castle was carefully dismantled, each stone being mapped for replacement and the entire castle removed from its island site to prevent it being submerged as the Galloway Hydro-electric scheme developed. This involved damming the loch at its northern end to raise the level of water in the loch to supply water for this major and very innovative project. Today, the remains of the castle can still be viewed on its island site and the waters around it still retain remnants of what was an illustrious and largely hidden past which saw this part of Ayrshire playing a pivitol role in history of the nation.

On April 19, 1966, Jim Buchanan, 17, of Dalmellington was fishing on the east side of the loch adjacent to the ruins of Portmark. He was accompanied by his friend, the late George Tulip. In casting his line he stumbled and fell. His hand landed on the edge of what he discovered was an old double-handled urn. He unearthed it from the stones at the loch edge and was amazed to find that it contained 1,187 ancient coins. Later examination of the hoard would reveal that many came from the 13th and 14th centuries including some from the period of the rule of John Balliol (Regent 1292 - 1296) and Robert the Bruce (1274 - 1329), surely the greatest of all Scottish heroes. These coins were given into the care of the National Museum of Scotland. They were able to tell Jim that the entire hoard would have been equivalent to the wages for one year of a Master Stone Mason. Could they have been hidden by a Loch Doon Stone Mason for safekeeping? Remember that these coins date to a time when the South of Scotland was subject to regular incursion by English forces under Edward I (1272 – 1307) and his son and heir, Edward II, who continued to wage war implacably against the Scots. This, then, was another indication of early human activity around the loch. No doubt even more surprising artefacts remain to be discovered by those who follow in our footsteps.

Breathes there the man with soul so dead,
Who never to himself hath said,
This is my own, my native land!

Breathes There The Man
Sir Walter Scott

CHAPTER 3
THE LOCH DOON FIASCO

Loch Doon has remained controversial throughout history. It was at South West Scotland's largest loch in September 1916 that the most astonishing plan was hatched to create a School of Aerial Gunnery, which would make Loch Doon into a seaplane base. The aim of the aerial gunnery school was to train pilots in target practice. It was intended that planes would take off from the loch and fly over a moving target range, which ran along the eastern flanks of the loch.

Loch Doon was chosen for this project for several reasons. First of all, it was in a relatively remote area, which could be easily guarded. Importantly, the loch was large enough for landing seaplanes. Secondly, there was also an area of flat land nearby on the west side of the loch, which could be used as an airfield and would house all the extensive support services for the School of Aerial Gunnery. Those planning this major engineering project seem to have been totally ignorant of the extreme difficulty of the terrain around the loch and the poor weather conditions prevailing in the area for much of the year.

Of the attempts to bring this strange idea to fruition Wilson remarked: " .. it is difficult to understand how any man, however ignorant, could conceive the idea of making Loch Doon into a seaplane base. Yet the idea was conceived; and what is more it was carried out, with a dogged obstinacy in face of undreamt-of difficulties and at a great cost to the lieges and much heartbreak to many." The reference to heartbreak refers to the suicide of the niece of Mrs McAdam of Craigengillan, Dalmellington. Craigengillan was commandeered by the armed forces during this project and Mrs McAdam's niece was apparently so upset at the hurt caused her aunt, that she took her own life.

However, like most failed projects there were also benefits. In the case of the Loch Doon scandal, the one positive result was that some 3,000 men including German prisoners-of-war were set to work on this massive engineering project which included building an access road to Loch Doon. McAlpine was ordered to commence the major road-building and engineering works in connection with the proposed seaplane base in September 1916 and this was carried out with haste and great success. However, of the aerial gunnery project, the result was inevitable from the outset. As Wilson highlighted, it was a total failure and a very expensive and ill-conceived project. Fortunately, Loch Doon was left with a fine minor road from Mossdale on the A713 road to the castle at the head of the loch. Indeed it was said to be one of the finest roads in Ayrshire at that time. Those travelling the Loch Doon road today would hardly agree, but of course the volume of traffic, including heavy forestry vehicles, and the popularity of Loch Doon as a tourist attraction, has increased traffic to

To sum up all: be merry, I advise;
And as we're merry, may we still be
wise!

Address spoken by Miss Fontenelle
Robert Burns

Loch Doon frozen over near to the Dam. Mrs May Mulholland and her daughter Eve of Polnessan. Note the concrete columns in the background which can still be seen on the east side of the loch.

Loch Doon dam on 15th June 2004 when the loch was incredibly low.

a level which those early road-builders could never have imagined.

A critic of the Loch Doon scheme from the very outset was Lt-Gen Sir Spencer Ewart of Craigcleuch, Langholm, who, in addition to living in the region, was General Officer Commanding Scotland from 1914 to 1918. It was said that Gen. Ewart also had a good knowledge of aviation matters and apparently he had actually met the Wright Brothers, during 1908-09 when he was Director of Military Operations at the War Office. In an unpublished auto-biography, quoted by Connon, he says:

"I was personally opposed to Loch Doon being selected as a site for such a range, because I realised the enormous sums which would be involved in the making of roads and approaches to it. Moreover, any local idiot could have informed the Army Council that a narrow and confined loch, situated at such a high elevation, was bound to be frozen and therefore useless for hydroplanes in the winter. Nobody in Whitehall would listen to my remonstrations and something over a million pounds, I believe, was wasted before this senseless project was abandoned. No such scandalous waste of public money was equalled, I imagine, anywhere else in the war and those responsible should, in my opinion, have been tried by Court Martial and removed from the service for incapacity. "

General Ewart clearly felt very strongly about the wisdom of this whole project and he was also acutely aware of the human cost of taking forward plans to build the School of Aerial Gunnery. He writes: *"The saddest thing about this melancholy business was the suicide of Mrs McAdam's niece, who lived with her at Craigengillan House (near Dalmellington), as a companion. She had appealed piously but vainly that officers should not be quartered upon the mansion where her aunt had just undergone an operation, and finally, poor girl, made away with herself. How the war office hushed up this disgraceful episode, I do not know. I even declined to sign the order quartering troops upon Craigengillan. Who signed it I never heard. While at Loch Doon I inspected some huts which had been built for a detachment of Royal Flying Corps and also the quarters provided for the Royal Engineers at Patna, Waterside and Dalmellington. I discussed with officers on the spot the question of sending a number of German Prisoners of War to act as a working party and selected a suitable site for an encampment."*

In fact the officers recollections are not entirely accurate when it comes to the suicide of the young lady. Mrs McAdam's sister had sent her daughter, Lavinette out of harms way from the war in France, to reside with her aunt at Craigengillan. The relationships between Mrs McAdam and Lavinette was destined not to be a happy one. With the activity of the military at Loch Doon, officers were billeted at Craigengillan. At age 20, Lavinette fell pregnant to one of these officers and Mrs McAdam had him ousted, which further upset and distressed her niece. Indeed local information is that Mrs McAdam made Lavinette's life hell thereafter. The young girl, only 20, was far from her home and

Black Craig and Coran of Portmark are seen from Loch Doon dam. Note the concrete pillars on the east side of the loch. These were built for the School of Ariel Gunnery during the Great War.

The extensive works in Dalmellington also involved building an airfield at Bogton on the north west edge of the village. This land had also been requisitioned and despite the best efforts of Mrs McAdam, a railway line was laid from the village to a railhead at Dalfarson through the grounds of Craigengillan Estate with the railhead lying across the valley and in sight of Craigengillan House. The railhead was about 1 mile short of the loch. All materials for the construction work was taken to Dalfarson from Dalmellington by light locomotive and thereafter transferred by lorry to the Loch. The remains of the buildings at Dalfarson can still be seen today. By February 1917, convoys of lorries were carrying 150 tons of goods every day from the Dalfarson railhead to the loch where a myriad of buildings were being erected and tons of concrete laid down on the west side of the loch. On the east side of the loch the visitor today can still see the large concrete blocks built to support a monorail.

loved ones in France. She was pregnant and living in what turned out to be a somewhat unwelcoming environment. Before the birth of the child, Lavinette went missing and was subsequently found dead having gassed herself in the estate gashouse adjacent to the Glessel Burn. The gashouse is now a substantial ruin and last produced gas for the estate around 1950. All in all a very sad episode in the fascinating story of Craigengillan.

No accurate figure for the Loch Doon fiasco was ever published, as far as is known. Lord Curzon, who was chairman of the Air Board in 1916 when the project was first sanctioned, was given the figure of £600,000 in reply to a question in the House of Lords.

Loch Doon castle taken on 15 June 2004.

The Hose girls of Dalmellington circa 1948
Back row: Margaret Hose (Hendry): Mary Hose (Reid)
Front: Annie Hose (Uriarte), Cathy Hose (Richmond) and Agnes Hose. Mary died in 2002. Margaret, Annie and Agnes still live in Dalmellington. Cathy lives in Kilmarnock.

However, J E Shaw, who was Clerk to Ayr County Council, in his book, Ayrshire 1745 – 1950, writes: *"More than £3 million had passed through the small bank at Dalmellington during the construction period at Loch Doon."* It can, therefore, be assumed that Shaw's estimate will have been much more accurate than the official published figure and indeed it only reflected movements through a small town bank, so the real cost of the School of Aerial Gunnery would have been astronomical.

All operations at Loch Doon were finally abandoned in January 1918. In short it was a disaster from start to finish. The targets moved too slowly to provide realistic training because the technology to support them was simply not available at that time. The Loch Doon airfield on the west side of the loch was impossible to drain because it had been constructed on a peat bog. Indeed more expense was added because the airfield had to be moved to a site at Bogton in Dalmellington. No one seemed to appreciate that this was too far away from Loch Doon for emergency landings. As locals had tried to explain from the outset, the weather was generally poor at Loch Doon, with too few days suitable

for flying. Winters could be simply appalling. So in January 1918 the Whitehall authorities were finally persuaded, probably in the main because of the spiralling costs, that this was indeed an ill-conceived project, inevitably doomed to failure from the outset.

The official report following this disastrous attempt at defeating the weather and mountains reported philosophically: *"Loch Doon and the country around it will soon return to the solitude and silence from which is was aroused by the introduction of thousands of men over a period of 15 months at a cost of hundreds of thousands of pounds of public money on an enterprise which was misconceived from the beginning, and which, even if once begun ought never to have been continued. Its name will be remembered as the scene of one of the most striking instances of wasted expenditure that our records can show."*

The report was also less than accurate in dramatically understating the cost as

"hundreds of thousands of pounds", when in reality the real costs ran into several million pounds. All the extensive buildings at Loch Doon, including a 400 seat cinema, were demolished and the land was largely returned to its former state. However, anyone visiting Loch Doon today should look carefully and at various points along its western fringes there is still extensive evidence of two years of frantic work by thousands of men. Look to the eastern shore and the evidence is even clearer of the support pillars on which the monorail would run the length of the loch. The lands around Beoch Farm also provide evidence of the extensive building programme undertaken from 1916 – 1917 with concrete foundations still visible today. However, the Loch Doon road is effectively, the only lasting legacy of what was one of Scotland's major engineering projects of the First World War. Nowadays, people who are aware of what is rightly called the Loch Doon scandal, can only wonder at the power of the military authorities, able to persuade government to finance a scheme which was a total fiasco from start to finish. So, Loch Doon can indeed tell many stories ancient and modern.

In Ploughman phrase, 'God send you speed.'
Still daily to grow wiser;
And may ye better reck the rede,
Than ever did th' adviser!

Epistle To A Young Friend
Robert Burns

CHAPTER 4

LOCH DOON SPITFIRE

The Second World War also brought another personal tragedy to the tranquil and relatively remote waters of Ayrshire's Loch Doon. Between 19th August 1941 and 1st January 1942, the 312 Czechoslovak Fighter Squadron was based at RAF Ayr at Heathfield. The base was busy with aircrew training, organised to very tight schedules. Inevitably, corners had to be cut to ensure that pilots were always available to fight the enemy. There was no time to instill in the pilots the finer points of airmanship. Only countless hours of flying experience in all weather conditions could ever achieve that. This was far from ideal, but the incessant demand for pilots and aircraft, meant it was part of the grim reality of military life in the war over the skies of Britain. Once basic flying skills were achieved it was likely that the next step would be operational patrols, which could involve the pilot in dog-fights with the enemy.

This was a time of tension for everyone. The sense of urgent preparation for engagement with the enemy was in the front of people's minds, not least those serving in the RAF in Ayrshire. They had to be ready for action. The war-machine was beginning to move into top gear, the objective of the RAF being to train as many pilots as possible to defend the country from the next onslaught from the Luftwaffe.

At the peak of the Battle of Britain 30 Hurricane units fought alongside 18 Spitfire and 10 "other fighter" squadrons. Indeed the Hurricane was said to be easier to repair quickly, because of the simpler, more robust structure than the advanced stressed-skin of the Spitfire. The Hurricane also had a much more robust, wider track undercarriage and hence easier take-off and landing characteristics than the Spitfire or the principal German opponent, the BF 109. This latter feature was of considerable importance to young British pilots, who were joining operational squadrons following hurried and limited training. Indeed as any aviation buff will tell, the Spitfire squadrons, were seen by many as hogging the glory, but were in fact very much in the minority. According to the RAF's Battle of Britain web site, the role of the Hurricane overshadowed the other flying defenders of Britain: "A total of 1,715 Hurricanes flew with Fighter Command during the period of the battle, far in excess of all other British fighters combined. It is estimated that its pilots were credited with four-fifths of all enemy aircraft destroyed in the period July - October 1940."

The military commanders were all too well aware that this was a looming battle, which would be won or lost in the air. Having pilots trained to the highest standard possible was a largely unattainable objective. In reality the available time-scale, all-too-often only allowed for a very basic level of training for many of the young airmen. They were then pushed to the frontline engaging the

Death, oft I've fear'd thy fatal blow!
Now fond I bare my breast;
O, do thou kindly lay me low
With him I love, at rest!

A Mother's Lament
Robert Burns

Loch Doon and a warning to caravanners not to park too close to the waters edge. The ruins of Eriff Farm, abandoned in the early 1900s, can be seen top right.

Pilot Officer Frantisek Hekl.

enemy in the unforgiving skies above Britain. Many would go on to become distinguished pilots, honing their skills at the sharp end of battle. Conversely, the vagaries of inadequate aircraft maintenance and ill-prepared pilots meant that for many, their fate was virtually sealed, the skies being totally unforgiving of human error by pilots and engineers. The position was exactly the same for the Pilot Officers being trained at RAF Ayr.

On 25th October 1941, Pilot Officer Frantisek Hekl, a young Czeck airman took off from RAF Ayr at Heathfield on a routine training flight which would take him over the Ayrshire and Galloway Hills. He was piloting a Supermarine Spitfire P7540 powered by the famous and very powerful Rolls Royce Merlin XII engine. This was one of many training missions, but Hekl was not to know that it would be his very last. He was proud, too, of his role and his aircraft. The Spitfire's reputation was assured. It had proved its worth in the Battle of Britain the year before. Later that day his plane was spotted crashing into Loch Doon near to Craigencoln Hill. It lay undiscovered for 40 years at a depth of about 12 metres. A subsequent search of the loch, which lasted for six weeks, failed to find any trace of Pilot Officer Hekl or the tragic Spitfire.

With the passage of time and the secrecy of war, the Spitfire crash was largely forgotten by all but a few folk. However, in 1976 Dumfries and Galloway Sub-Aqua Club and Dumfries and Galloway Aircraft Recovery Group, greatly encouraged by two dynamic leaders in David Greenwood and Bruce Robertson, took on the momentous task of searching for and recovering the Loch Doon Spitfire. This dedicated group worked diligently for a staggering six years in a co-ordinated search of the crash scene in the most dangerous and difficult conditions at great depths. Most groups would have given up the task, but there was a gritty determination by the team to succeed.

At the outset they were fortunate in that they were able to trace two eye-witnesses to the crash in 1941. Mr E McCormick of Dalry and Mr Bob Howatson, both saw the plane come down in the water in an area between Cullendoch and Craigencoln hills. Bob, was 12 years of age at the time. He was the son of Quintin and Queenie Howatson, the boatman/caretaker and cook at Finlas Lodge at Loch Doon. They were frantically alerted to the tragedy by the shocked Bob, who had seen the tragic event unfold as he happily played near the scene. As the plane flew low over the loch the pilot banked his aircraft and his starboard wing struck the surface, causing the aircraft to catapult along the surface and crash into Loch Doon.

Quinton Howatson sprang into action knowing that time was of the essence. He set off at speed cycling northwards the half mile to Beoch Farm, where the only telephone in the area was located. From there he made contact with Sergeant Joss of Dalmellington Police and made the grim report. The Sergeant immediately alerted the RAF and the emergency services swung into action at Loch Doon. On arrival at the scene, and for several weeks thereafter, the RAF team used Finlas Lodge as their base in what turned out to be a fruitless search for the wreckage of the Spitfire and her missing pilot.

Over 30 years later, McCormick and Howatson were able to assist in the search for the lost Spitfire. They pinpointed the crash scene with great accuracy independently of each other. To the great delight of the searchers, they identified an area within 100 metres of each other and this was the catalyst for the eventual recovery of what has become known as the Loch Doon Spitfire. It can be speculated that the pilot was perhaps pushing the aircraft beyond his novice ability to control it. There may have been catastrophic engine failure. The truth of the circumstances of the crash will never be fully known, although major parts of the aircraft were later recovered.

The difficult search work by enthusiastic volunteers continued year on year with limited success. Nevertheless their commitment was rewarded when on 15th May 1982, diver Barry Barkworth, discovered the fuselage of the Spitfire. The excitement at this positive result was explosive after a search lasting six years, but the find had to be kept secret until the MOD gave permission to lift the fuselage. This was subsequently recovered together with the engine, wings and hydraulic gear. Although the fuselage was in good condition, damage to the cockpit was severe. This was an amazing feat of endurance by the divers. Indeed it was estimated that 109 individual divers made 567 separate dives and a total of 337 hours were spent underwater searching the crash area.

Sadly, despite the recovery of extensive wreckage, there was no trace of the remains of Pilot Officer Frantisek Hekl, whose last resting place remains in the murky depths of Loch Doon far from his home and family in Czechoslovakia. A small cairn on the loch side marks the spot near to where this brave airman died.

The Spitfire can with some justification be called the most famous aircraft of all time, although the key role of the Hurricane has never been fully acknowledged. The public perception is that the Spitfire almost single-handedly saved Britain from German invasion. The reality is that the Hurricane certainly played a greater and more successful role in the conflict. The Spitfire was designed by Reginald Mitchell. He was dying of cancer, but lived long enough to see the

prototype fly for the first time in 1936. It was the first all metal stressed skin fighter to go into production in Britain and was developed just in time to help the redoubtable Hawker Hurricane save Britain from disaster in the Battle of Britain in the late summer of 1940.

312 (Czeck) Squadron was established on 5th September 1940 at RAF Duxford and was disbanded on 22nd September 1945 in Ceske, Budejovice, Czechoslovakia. It is also sobering to realise that 116,000 men and women of the Air Forces of the Commonwealth gave their lives during the Second World War (1939 – 1945). Like Pilot Officer Hekl, many of them lie in foreign fields and the memory of their sacrifice is sadly, largely forgotten with the passage of time.

The tragic Loch Doon Spitfire P7540 is now being reconstructed and can be seen at Dumfries and Galloway Aviation Group Museum of Flight situated in the outskirts of Dumfries. A chat with any of the enthusiastic volunteers at this

Czeck Squadran at RAF Ayr, 1943. Pilot Officer Hekl, second from left front row.

outstanding museum will prove very worthwhile. Interestingly, in 2004 the nephew of Frantisek Hekl visited the Museum of Flight at Dumfries. In what turned out to be a very moving visit for him and the museum staff, he was shown the remains of the Spitfire and pictures of the Czeck Squadron based at Ayr. He was able to quietly pay tribute to an uncle whom he had never met, but whose proud story he knew very well indeed. Importantly, the visit to see the Spitfire will be a special and lasting memory for the young Czeck and he will pass on the story to those who follow in his family footsteps. A rather fitting end to yet another sad episode at Loch Doon.

When you go home.
Tell them of us, and say,
For your tomorrow.
We gave our to-day.
Kohima Epitaph

CHAPTER 5
BLUE PETER CRASHES ON CAIRNSMORE

As a young man I was fascinated by the grey hills of Galloway which rose so majestically from above the southern end of Loch Doon. As often as possible I would be off on the most enjoyable sojourns to the Merrick by way of the Pulskaig Burn which runs between Mullwharchar and Dungeon Hill leading to lonely Loch Enoch, a place of happy memory. Great days were spent walking from the Tunskeen Bothy by way of Shalloch-on-Minnoch along the hill tops with names to conjure with - Tarfessock, Kirriereoch and up the narrow and often wind-swept Little Spear, to the crest of the Merrick. Here I could savour wonderful views, not least of which looking down on Loch Enoch with its silver sand gleaming in the sun. On the way back to Loch Doon I would drop in to have a cup of tea and a chat with Davy Wilson, who at that time lived in a very comfortable hut near to Loch Head, near the Gala Lane. Davy was always pleased to have a visitor and made walkers very welcome. Happy days!

Backhill of Bush, said to be the loneliest house in Galloway, was to be a regular haunt over the years. Once occupied by a wonderful character who was a shepherd, Alex Renton, who spent the Autumn of his life in Dalmellington, he was later Shepherd at Burnhead Farm located adjacent to the remains of Corbie Craigs rows at the top of Dunaskin Glen. Alex was able to recount many an interesting story about walkers visiting the area in the post-war period. On one occasion three lads arrived at Backbush intent on spending the night a few miles down the Dee Valley at Black Laggan on the southern edge of Loch Dee. However, the happy trio were unnerved by the night shadows, winds rustling through the trees and the ghostly atmosphere of low clouds and in the early hours arrived back at Backbush where the Rentons fed them and gave them a bed for the night.

As a Mountain Bothy, Backhill o' Bush was to be an ideal base for many memorable trips to Mullwharchar, Dungeon Hill, Craignaw and explorations around Loch Enoch. Heading across from the bothy inevitably meant wet feet. A direct line from the Backbush meant crossing the floating bog known as the Silver Flow to reach the two Dungeon Lochs. However, the dramatic scenery of Dungeon and Craignaw Hills more than compensated for wet feet. The Rhinns of Kells running from Black Craig, Coran of Portmark. Bow, Meul and Carlin's Cairn were flat-topped rolling hills, but with a precipitous and dangerous eastern flank. However, they had the added advantage of affording the most magnificent views of the Murrwharchar and Merrick ranges.

Cairnsmore of Carsphairn fits into the category of a long, bulky scree-faced hill sitting 797 metres above sea level. It is largely bereft of any inspiring features apart from large areas of scree, but has some of the finest dry-stane dykes in Scotland. Like other tops in the area, it does afford magnificent views in all directions. My first visit was in 1966 walking in from the village of Carsphairn. Resting in the cooling breeze after my exertions, one could really savour the tranquility of the day and the superb views of the surrounding countryside. I had no idea at that time that just a short distance from where I rested, a wartime spitfire, Blue Peter No AD540, crashed in 1942 tragically taking the life of her young airman, Pilot Officer David Hunter Blair. The Spitfire and Hurricane were of the legendary group of aircraft that proved so effective in the Battle of Britain.

On May 23, 1942, Jim McGarva, then a lad of 19 years, was a shepherd at Clenoch and was busily working in the Valley of Carsphairn. He was grafting away in poor weather conditions digging drainage ditches, hard back-breaking work. The fact that it was a pretty miserable day, made the work all the more loathsome, but it had to be done. Suddenly, he heard the echoing sound of an aircraft overhead. Looking skyward, a small plane ominously appeared through the dark storm clouds, spinning gently as if the pilot was unaware of the impending danger of Cairnsmore of Carsphairn.

As he watched mesmerized, it finally came to earth with a shattering explosion on Cairnsmore, the echo of the shattering crash reverberating round the hills. His first thoughts were of disbelief. Could this really be happening? He immediately discarded his spade and began frantically running, his heart pounding as if about to burst, in the direction of the stricken aircraft, about a kilometre away. He recalled: "I was looking to pull folk out of the aircraft. It was upside down with its tail sticking in the air and fortunately it wasn't on fire, just kind of steaming and hissing as if it was angry at crashing. I could see the cockpit clearly, its glass all broken, but to my astonishment there was nobody inside. It was then, as I looked back, that I noticed way in the distance on Dugland Hill far across the valley, what I thought was smoke and I began to run once again."

What Jim had taken to be smoke was in fact the parachute of Spitfire pilot, David Hunter Blair, billowing in the wind immediately behind the spot where Jim had been working. He never saw the parachute descend to earth because he had been so busy working digging drains. After hearing the crash his only concern was to reach the crashed aircraft as quickly as possible. So, he set off in direction of the downed Spitfire, running like he had never run before. It was, therefore, wholly understandable that he did not see Hunter Blair's parachute descend immediately behind where he was working in the valley on the adjacent Dugland Hill. If only he had looked backward he would have seen the stricken airman falling to the ground.

When he eventually reached the flowing parachute he was sorely vexed that a body of an airman was lying at the end of the parachute lines. He immediately set about cutting away the parachute and he carefully covered the lifeless body with the parachute. Breathing heavily through extreme exertion and shock, he

Spitfire over Cairnsmore of Carsphairn.

ran and walked the three miles to where his motor cycle was parked and sped at break-neck speed to St Johns Town of Dalry where he reported the crash to the local police. A rescue team was assembled as quickly as possible and left for the crash site arriving there some three hours later. The doctor confirmed that Pilot Officer David Hunter Blair was indeed dead and his remains were subsequently recovered.

During that fateful journey to Dalry and on many subsequent occasions, Jim began to reflect on what might have happened. Had the young pilot's parachute been fully inflated as he hit the ground? Had he wrestled with the controls of the doomed aircraft until it was simply too late to save his own life? Had he suffered from oxygen starvation and sank into unconsciousness? If that were indeed the case, how did he manage to abandon the aircraft? There were no obvious injuries to the body with the exception of a trickle of blood coming from the nose. Unfortunately, Jim had no knowledge of basic first aid and was not

Ralph Davidson at the scene of the remains of the crashed spitfire on Cairnsmore of Carsphairn.

even able to check for a pulse, but all the signs were that the pilot was lifeless. This episode had a lasting effect on Jim McGarva who later lived in Waterside near Dalmellington and he bitterly regretted that he was unable to do more and perhaps have saved the life of the spitfire pilot. If only he had turned and look backwards when he heard the distinctive sound of the doomed Spirtfire. The likelihood is that the young airman was already dead when he hit the ground and there were certainly no obvious signs of life when McGarva reached the stricken flyer.

A recovery team from the RAF subsequently attended at the crash scene and removed the wings using a horse to drag them down the hillside to their base at Moorbrock Farm for recovery by the RAF.

However, 50 years elapsed before the final remains of Spitfire Blue Peter were recovered and taken to the Museum of Flight, Dumfries where they can be seen today with a reconstruction of Spitfire Blue Peter. On May 1, 1992, Ralph J Davidson, an aircraft enthusiast and then chairman of the Scottish Branch of the Spitfire Society, received a request from the BBC seeking information about the crash site of Blue Peter. They hoped to make a 50th anniversary feature for the BBC's famous children's programme of the same name.

The intrepid Davidson visited Cairnsmore of Carsphairn in September 1992 with a BBC production team who had travelled north to film the first efforts to locate the crash site of AD540 Blue Peter. Included in the search party was Andy Adamson, 80, who as a boy had seen the aircraft on the hillside. John Lesley, famous presenter of BBCs Blue Peter, was also there and the producer was Bill Locke. The weather was very poor and after searching unsuccessfully for five hours, the producer decided that they had sufficient film for their purposes. However, this was the beginning of many visits to Cairnsmore by Ralph Davidson and friends who were determined to uncover the mystery of Blue Peter. Davidson eventually teamed up with Jim Bell, another former shepherd who remembered the aircraft very clearly being recovered by the RAF. He had witnessed what he presumed to be the wings being dragged down the hill by a horse during the recovery process. The rest of the remains of Blue Peter were buried near the crash site on the hillside by the RAF team, a common practice with aircraft marooned in remote hill

areas. The Galloway hills has seen many such aircraft crashes over the years.

Encouraged by this further positive information Davidson assembled some friends to help with the search and you can imagine their sheer elation on finding the unmistakable sight of a piece of aircraft aluminum on Cairnsmore. Using metal detectors they were soon able to locate the crash site and were satisfied that this was indeed the final resting place of Spitfire, Blue Peter. Strangely enough the date of this find was staggering in that it happened to be May 23, 1993, exactly 51 years to the very day of Blue Peter's demise and very near to the time of the actual crash.

The problem now facing Ralph Davidson and his dedicated team was how to go about salvaging what was left of Blue Peter. The following three weekends were spent digging for wreckage and they found it in abundance. Ralph managed to enlist a large number of volunteers to help with the mammoth task. The BBC also returned to film the recovery operation. Among the early finds was the discovery of the port wing and aircraft's cannon magazines. Both magazines were complete with complement of 20mm ammunition of 60 rounds per magazine.

Later they were to recover a Hispano cannon, a round still in the breach, the guns probably never having been fired in anger by Blue Peter's young pilot. Further examination showed that one of the gun barrels was damaged, probably accounting for it being buried rather than recovered. What had previously been thought to be the wings of the aircraft recovered by the RAF in 1942 proved to be wrong. It was actually the wing tips which, strangely enough, had been recovered near to the body of the young airman, and far from the main wreckage site. Perhaps the aircraft had begun to break-up prior to hitting the ground. No one will ever know for certain. In a second burial site some 200 yards from the main crash site, the team recovered the oil tank, cockpit section, and lower fuel tank. These were recovered from three sites in the same peat bog. Clearly the RAF had chosen to bury these at a lower site because of the soft ground, making disposal much easier.

Incredibly, in just five weekends of frantic work, sometimes in dreadful weather conditions, the wreckage of Blue Peter lay at the second recovery site. All that remained at the main crash site was the once mighty Merlin engine. All the wreckage was bagged in preparation for removal to the Museum of Flight, Dumfries.

Ralph Davidson recalled: "On July, 12 I was standing at the recovery site when I heard the sound of a giant Sea King helicopter from HMS Gannet, Prestwick. The thud of the blades reverberated along the valley as it descended on Cairnsmore. The helicopter pilot flew over the crash site as tribute to the fallen airman before returning and hovering over the site and two crewman jumped out to prepare the load for the flight out. This was the agreed means of transporting the remains of Blue Peter from her lonely hillside

Grave of David Gaspart Hunter Blair who died in the Spitefire crash on Cairnsmore of Carsphairn. He is buried in the grounds of Blairquan, Straiton.

resting place. Cargo nets were dropped from the aircraft and three loads of wreckage were subsequently flown to the A713 at Drumjohn for subsequent transportation by road to Dumfries."

This was not the end of the tale as far as Ralph Davidson was concerned. Early on during the search he had decided that a memorial should be erected on Dugland Hill at the point where Pilot Officer Hunter Blair had lost his life. He felt it important that hill walkers passing that way might remember the sad event that occurred all those years ago on

Cairnsmore. Another memorial was subsequently erected near the main crash site for the same reason. The inscription was simple and appropriate. It read: *"Near this spot on the 23rd May, 1942, PO David Hunter Blair, aged 19, a Scot from Ayrshire, was mortally wounded after parachuting from Spitfire AD540 Blue Peter. He died that others might live."* The inscription finished poignantly with the words, *"Lest We Forget,"* acknowledging not only the loss of one man, but the many sacrifices during the Second World War by those who flew Spitfires, Hurricanes and other aircraft. Fittingly, at the inauguration of the memorial, Ralph Davidson as part of his tribute to David Hunter Blair read this line, *"Do not despair for Johnny head in air,"* from a famous war poem and this was followed by a minute's silence in honour of the fallen airman.

Fittingly, at this special service of remembrance, two spitfires flew over Cairnsmore. It is often said that a spitfire is heard before it is seen, and this proved to be the case on that memorable day. The small company gathered on the remote Galloway hill, including the brother of the fallen pilot, heard the roar of the distinctive engines, looked up and there were two spitfires proudly saluting a lost comrade. The next pass was directly in front of the party, the wartime veteran aircraft disappearing eastwards.

They quickly returned from the east, only this time Squadron Leader Martin flew directly over the memorial stone at barely 100 feet. Ralph Davidson recalled: "Those who witnessed this very moving tribute felt the hair on their neck stand on end with sheer joy seeing such an appropriate tribute to a lost airman. It was a very special occasion for me and those who helped in the search for Blue Peter." There were many tears of joy and thanksgiving shed that day as the gathered company watched the departing silhouettes of a bygone age as the sound of their Merlin engines faded as they disappeared south. Once again the lonely valley of Cairnsmore became silent. Those fortunate enough to have witnessed this moving spectacle will forever recall that special day in the lonely hills of Galloway. A special debt of gratitude is also owed to a determined man who finally revealed the resting place of Blue Peter - Ralph J Davidson, a man of vision, determination and great compassion.

The soger frae the war returns,
The sailor frae the main,
But I hae parted frae my love,
Never to meet again, my dear -
Never to meet again.

It Was A' For Our Rightfu King
Robert Burns

David Hunter Blair as a young lad, perhaps thinking about becoming a famous aviator.

David Hunter Blair aged 19 in 1942 with his spitfire.

CHAPTER 6
NESS GLEN TO CRAIGENGILLAN

The River Doon issues from the northern end of the loch at the once magnificent dam, which now seems to have seen better days. For nearly a mile its course is through a remarkably wild and picturesque Ness Glen where it leaps and tumbles in a picturesque white water descent. Perpendicular cliffs, sometimes scarcely 50 feet apart, rise to a height of around 200 feet on either bank.

The hand of Nature everywhere pervades,
And blends the barren rocks and verdant shades

Ness Glen
Robert Hetrick

A footpath has been cut on the west bank of the river, and in the latter part of the 19th century Ness Glen was one of the most beautiful and wild spots in the south of Scotland. Indeed the glen was such a popular tourist attraction that it could boast having its own curator who took parties along its narrow route and explained the bird and plant life to visitors. In the late 1800s and well into the early 20th century, charabanc outings came from all over the West of Scotland to visit Loch Doon and enjoy guided tours through Ness Glen. Over the last 30 years the glen has become impassable due to landslides, erosion and fallen trees. But it remains an area of outstanding natural beauty which did inspire generations of visitors. In the opening poem of his little volume

published in 1826, Robert Hetrick, the blacksmith-poet of Dalmellington, thus describes Ness Glen:

"Doon issuing from her slumbering bed of rest,
Is downward through the rockly tunnel prest,
Then dash'd against yon shelvy, pointed rock.
Which, unmolested, stands the furious shock,
And turns the torrent to the other side,
Which, in its turn, resists the furious tide;
Here dashing on the precipices steep;
There boiling in the dreadful caverns deep;
Now madly raging o'er the ragged linn,
Mocking the voices of thunder its din;
Bathing the margins with foamy spray;
And thus the tortured waters pass away,
Leaving the caverns, linns, and rocks behind,
For banks and channels of a gentler kind,
Where the woods and lawns alternate please the eye;
With bowers and cottages and streamlets nigh –
Where music swells in ilka leafy grove,
In all the charms of harmony and love;
And fair Barbeth stands clad in summer green,
Adds lustre to the wild, romantic scene."

Hetrick is a fair example of a village poet of whom there were many in Ayrshire. Inspired by Robert Burns, he brought his own poetic offerings before the public.

Come let us stray our gladsome way,
And view the charms of Nature;
The rustling corn, the fruited thorn,
And ilka happy creature.

Now Westlin Winds
Robert Burns

Magnificent Ness Glen near to Loch Doon. This was taken about 1903 and may be Mrs Charlotte McAdam (Tilke). The Ness Glen pathway is currently being rebuilt so that in due course the public can enjoy this scenic walk through a classic Scottish gorge.

35

The gamekeepers house at Craigengillan, no longer extant. The house was rased to the ground in the late 1950s. The last occupant was a Mr Steel, who was found dead in the house.

Craigengillan was a large and very busy country house. This is probably 1890s with the domestic staff posing for a photograph.

None of his poems rise above mediocrity, but he was an unassuming man with a genuine love for his native Doon, which finds expression in many of his pleasing lines, winning him great local acclaim.

Dalmellington, too, had particular associations with Robert Burns as well as many admirers of his work such as Hetrick. Craigengillan is the impressive mansion referred to by its former name, Barbeth, in Hetrick's poem and sits in extensive lands about 2 miles from the village along a private road. At the time when the bard was writing his poetry, John McAdam of Craigengillan was addressed in the poem To Mr McAdam of Craigen-Gillan:

"I'll cock my nose aboon them a',
I'm roos'd by Craigen-Gillan."

McAdam had sent Burns "an obliging letter in the commencement of his career as a poet," a letter of which Burns was very proud:

Sir, o'er a gill I gat your card,
I trow it made me proud;
'See whas taks notice o' the bard'!
I lap and cry'd fu' loud.

McAdam was an innovative landowner and he brought a "dyker" from the north to instruct the people of his estates in the building of stone fences, an affair to which Burns alludes in the verse:

An' when those legs to guid, warm kail
Wi' welcome canna bear me,
A lee dykeside, a sybow tail,
An' barley scone shall cheer me.

John McAdam was born in 1700 and succeeded to the estate in 1724 and developed the lands. He is said to have been fair in business dealings. It was this John McAdam who built Craigengillan, earlier called Berbeth. He was acquainted with James Boswell and he is mentioned in his famous journal. John McAdam had one son and two daughters. In the final stanza of the poem, Burns refers to John McAdam's son, Col. Quinton McAdam as "Young Dunaskin's Laird." Quinton was also referred to in the poem, *Second Heron Election Ballad*, as 'o' lads no the wars.' In a letter from Edinburgh dated, 11 January 1787 Burns made reference to one of John McAdam's two daughters as "the beauty-famed and wealth-celebrated Miss McAdam, our countrywoman."

With such connections it might reasonably be supposed that Burns may indeed have visited Craigengillan at some stage and he would certainly have passed through Dalmellington on his travels on more than one occasion. Indeed McKay records (page 193 - *Burns a Biography*) that the poet was in New Cumnock on 18 August 1786. "From there he rode westwards through Dalmellington to Maybole arriving there about Friday, 25 August. There he stayed with his old school chum Willie Niven, visiting subscribers in the district and collecting money for copies of his book."

Perhaps he did take the opportunity of visiting his benefactor at Craigengillan on route to Maybole. The two pretty daughters would have been a real attraction to the poet, but we will never know for certain. However, Burns was not one to turn down an opportunity to make his mark with powerful people in the upper echelons of society and a night or two spent in the opulent surroundings of Craigengillan would doubtless have appealed to the poet. What is certain, though, is that his legend is to be felt in Ayrshire, the heartland of Burns Country.

Craigengillan is seen to best advantage from the Loch Doon road just before it descends to the Gaw Glen. The Gaw Glen was probably named for John Gaa who was born the son of a shepherd at Little Shalloch (OS77: 451029), for many years a ruin. John was a merchant in Dalmellington. It is said that he was a passenger in a coach crossing McClymont's Bridge, Dalmellington, when the horses shied and both coach and horses were capsized over the bridge into the Muck Burn. John Gaa survived but never quite recovered from the accident and died a short time later in November 1834, aged 77 years. He willed his money to convert his property into a free Reading Room for Dalmellington and to be supplied with newspapers and magazines. His family bible and fiddle were at one time in the care of Dalmellington District Council. It is said that the Gaa Trust owns feus on Carsphairn Road and Townhead Street and ground at Cathcartson including the site of the Bowling Green and property in High Main Street.

During 2001 - 2005 there began extensive renovations to Craigengillan under the guiding hand of its present owner, Mark Gibson, aimed at ensuring the building returns to a fitting condition for such a grand and historic mansion. Not only that, but Mark Gibson has generously opened up Craigengillan policies to the general public and has even built a new bridge spanning the River Doon at the foot of Ness Glen with ongoing work to replace the pathway through this charming gorge. In the late 1800s Ness Glen attracted huge numbers of visitors and the last precentor of Dalmellington Parish Church, William Hewitson, was employed as a guide to escort parties through the glen and explain its interesting flora and fauna. It was said that the birds would come to Hewitson and settle on his hand, such was his affinity with nature.

Craigengillan is very much a working estate and the visitor can enjoy horse riding, fishing and walking in these tranquil and invigorating policies. On certain occasions you can also enjoy listening to the music of the famous Dalmellington Band. This innovative landowner has also hosted major events such as boxing tournaments, weddings, fund raising dinners and other social functions in the grounds of the mansion house ensuring that the estate is moving with the times and helping to finance future developments. The estate has open days and hosts charity events such as sponsored walks, all aimed at encouraging people to enjoy, value and respect this attractive land.

There is also much credible information and local tradition to suggest that Craigengillan occasionally hosted foreign royals, British Prime Ministers and Cabinet Ministers, mainly in the first half

Frederick McAdam Cathcart with a rare family photograph taken in 1861-62 outside Craigengillan. What appears to be a little girl seven along is in fact a boy, Charles Cathcart.
(l to r in a straight line): (1) Jane McAdam Cathcart, wife of Quentin; (2) Frederick McAdam Cathcart, Jane's husband; (3) Louisa Cathcart, sister of Frederick; (4) Emily Cathcart, the daughter of Georgina; (5) Georgina, wife of George Cathcart of Inkerman fame and sister in law of Frederick; (6) Ann Cathcart, daughter of George and niece of Frederick; (7) Charles Cathcart, son of Elizabeth Douglas and Great Nephew of Frederick McAdam Cathcart; (8) Elizabeth Douglas, daughter of 3rd Earl and niece of Frederick; Louise Cathcart, daughter of Georgina and niece of Frederick.

of the 20th century. Many local people, whose relations are still alive today, worked at Craigengillan in 1900 - 1950 period when Mrs Charlotte McAdam was a noted socialite. Her then husband, Alexander Frederick McAdam died on 8 January 1901 and is buried in the family

vault in the old cemetery in Dalmellington. Mrs Charlotte McAdam had a special commemorative stained glass window placed in Dalmellington Parish Church in his honour. After his death she continued to host rich and famous visitors at Craigengillan.

Employees would have been privy to knowledge of important visitors over the years, but these were kept very quiet, although information was shared among family members. And of course, Craigengillan was very much out-of-bounds for locals, so the estate was in many ways ideal for those of political importance and social standing wishing to enjoy a peaceful period of respite in lovely surroundings with good fishing, shooting and walking.

Leslie Pike, the son of the chauffeur, spent his childhood at Craigengillan. He recalls that between 1921 - 1927 Stanley Baldwin (1867 - 1947), three times Prime Minister, was a visitor. The late Mary Johnstone of Burnton worked as a servant there full-time from 1928 - 1930 and for years afterwards on an occasional basis when the house had guests. She, too, was aware of many important people visiting Mrs McAdam.

It is reputed that about 1938 Mr Marr, gardener at Craigengillan, was working in the potting shed when he witnessed a heated exchange of views between two of the guests, talking in the garden

nearby. The subject was government policy towards Germany. The VIP guests were Neville Chamberlain, Prime Minister 1937 - 1940, and his foreign secretary (1938 - 1940), Lord Halifax, formerly Viceroy of India. They apparently enjoyed fishing on the Loch and River Doon. Prince Rainier III of Monaco (1923 - 2005) was often a guest at Craigengillan as a boy. After the Second World War it is known that Prince Rainier III made two further visits to Craigengillan. In 1949 he ascended the throne of Monaco and later caught the world's attention with his story-book marriage to actress Grace Kelly (1929 - 1982). In 1997, the Grimaldi family celebrated the 700th anniversary of its reign in Monaco. Mrs Charlotte McAdam (Tilke) originally from Dijon, France, was often a guest of the Grimaldi family when she wintered abroad. Probably through the Grimaldi connection, it is said that another royal,

King Gustav of Denmark also spent time at Craigengillan. No doubt there would be others, too, as Charlotte McAdam seems to have had a wide and influential sphere of relationships in high society with many friends in foreign aristocratic circles. Known informally as Lady McAdam in Dalmellington, she died in 1953 and is buried in the McAdam vault in the old Dalmellington cemetery.

Sir William Beardmore (1856 - 1936), later Lord Invernairn was also a frequent visitor. Beardmore attended Ayr Academy with one of the McAdam's and kept up this relationship in later life. During the 1930s there were many visitors to Craigengillan, including government ministers and officials and foreign aristocrats, there to enjoy the grouse shooting and fishing on Loch Doon and its famous river.

One interesting visitor was Lord Mitford,

his official title was Baron Resesdale. He was the rather eccentric father of the six famous Mitford sisters - Nancy, Diana, Unity, Jessica, Pamela and Deborah. His daughter Unity brought great notoriety on the family when she developed a close relationship with Adolf Hitler. Sister Diana married Oswald Mosley of the British Union of Fascists. The Oswalds were both arrested a few months after war began and joined other Natzi sympathizers in prison. Unusual in the extreme, they were allowed to share a cell and released just before the end of the war.

Diana and Unity appear to have had close links to the German high command. Diana's wedding to Mosley actually took place in Goebbel's drawing room. Later, when war was announced Unity was in Germany and attempted to commit suicide by shooting herself in the head. She was torn between her love of

England and Germany and saw death as the only answer. She survived and with the blessing of Hitler himself, was shipped back to England where she remained an invalid until her death in 1948.

It has often been postulated to what extent if any, Unity and Diana influenced Hitler. In fact Unity believed that Hitler was not only a great leader. To her he was a true genius, an almost God-like character who could do no wrong. Many believe that she was totally infatuated with Hitler and probably in love. Did Unity and Diana give the Nazis a tainted picture of England and its people and lead them to believe that the country was unwilling to fight or even sympathetic to the Nazi cause? Hitler may have seen Unity and Diana as important conduits for the Nazi cause. They were, after all, from an aristocratic English family, their father being a member of the House of

Lords and sister Nancy an influential writer. What were the true views of Lord Resesdale on Hitler and would he have had any private influence on cabinet ministers when in retreat at Craigengillan?

Conversely, Hitler may have been rather naive assuming that because the Mitfords were from the aristocracy that they and their family exerted influence over the government. Yet, such simplistic thinking did exist in the German High Command. No better example of their mistaken notions can be found than Rudolph Hess' mad flight, two years later. Apparently believing he could ask the sympathetic Duke of Hamilton to negotiate a peace, the Reich Minister parachuted into Scotland, landing near to Eaglesham village. He was quickly arrested. During his interrogation, Hess repeatedly demanded to speak to the "opposition party," of which he thought the Duke of Hamilton was a leader. In other words: as late as 1941, at least some in the German high command believed they enjoyed wide support in Britain.

So, does some tiny measure of the responsibility for World War II lie with the Unity and Diana Mitford? It will always be an intriguing but unanswerable question. Yet another fascinating link between important people in government, aristocrats from home and abroad and Dalmellington's Craigengillan House.

Craigengillan was also the setting for

another sad episode during the Great War. Mrs McAdam's niece, Lavinette, was packed off to Craigengillan from France for her own protection. She became pregnant by an officer billeted at the mansion. Lavinette was so debilitated by the affair that she committed suicide in the estate gasworks. She seems to have been broken-hearted at the officer being ousted from Craigengillan and being prohibited from having any contact with him. Local tradition passed down from estate staff has it that Mrs McAdam dealt rather severely and unfairly with her niece, culminating in the young lady taking her own life. A tragic affair indeed.

Craigengillan was to be the scene of two more tragic deaths. The body of Andrew McCutcheon, postman, High Main Street, Dalmellington, was recovered from the River Doon on 29 January 1936. The previous day two women had passed McCutcheon sitting on the bridge over the Doon just over 1 mile from the mansion. He was sitting on the bridge with his back to the river, his feet swinging as he was having a smoke. His bag and cape were sitting beside him on the parapet. A short time later a passing motorist on route to Craigengillan passed over the bridge and saw McCutcheons post bag and cape sitting neatly on the parapet of the bridge, but there was no signs of McCutcheon. He had completed his delivery of letters up to that point.

The police and postal authorities were immediately notified of the situation and a search was carried on along the banks of the River until darkness without finding any trace of the missing man. The following day the police arranged for the sluices at Loch Doon dam to be turned off allowing the level of water in the River Doon to fall significantly and McCutcheon's body was found in and recovered from the river about 100 metres downstream from the bridge. It is thought that he had lost his balance while seated on the bridge and fallen into the river. From that time until the present the only bridge over the River Doon on the main approach to Craigengillan has been called the Postman's Bridge, recalling this sad accident.

Two years later in 1938 Postman Lamb of Dalmellington, who lived at 16 Cathcartson drowned himself at the dam at Loch Doon. He took the toggle chord off his post bag, tied it round his ankles, climbed the dam wall and threw himself over. He was a single man suffering from depression. His body was later recovered. Personal tragedy seems to have been inextricably linked to Craigengillan.

Despite some sad events, the rich and famous and, of course, ordinary people have long enjoyed Loch Doon, some 5.5 miles long and about 1.5 miles broad. To many this is a magical area of outstanding scenic beauty, which regularly draws people back time and again. Visit the area and reflect on its history, ancient and modern, and picture in your minds eye the epic struggles which took place in this area over the centuries. Begin to imagine what it was like between 1916 - 1918 when it was a hive of activity with 3,000 men undertaking major public works in war-time. Here you are in the midst of living history and the area has earned the right to be preserved and managed in a way that will ensure that it remains largely unspoiled for the benefit of generations who will follow. Mark Gibson of Craigengillan is playing a key role in restoring the famous Ness Glen gorge footpath and showing astute management skills with the famous mansion and estate.

This area is very special. We simply need the wild country available to us, even if we do no more than drive to its edge and look in. For it is a means of reassuring ourselves of our sanity as creatures, a part of our geography of hope.

"Keep these places for your children and your children's children if you can: the more cities increase the more precious they will be." Octavia Hill, 1876.

I am the River Doon, whose name
To public notice has a claim,
For Burns' great exalted theme,
Of Lyric worth,
Has class'd me with his spreading fame
Throughout the earth.

The Petition of the River Doon
Robert Hetrick

Clockwise from top left:

Prince Rainier III of Monaco, a guest at Craigengillan House, Dalmellington;

Lord Halifax, Foreign Secretary (1938 - 40) in Chamberlain's government. He was a former Viceroy of India. He also visited Craigengillan House, Dalmellington; See chapter: Ness Glen to Craigengillan;

Neville Chamberlain, Prime Minister (1937 - 1940) was a visitor to Craigengillan. His wife was a cousin of Charlotte McAdam (Tilke). See chapter: Ness Glen to Craigengillan;

Charlotte McAdam (Tilk) was known locally as Lady McAdam. She was from Dijon, France and married Alexander Frederick McAdam of Craigengillan. He died aged 36 and she took over the running of the estate. She was a noted socialite and many royals, aristocrats and government ministers enjoyed the hospitality of Craigengillan, Dalmellington;

Sir William Beardmore (1856-1936) of William Beardmore & Co, was a frequent guest at Craigengillan to enjoy the walking and fishing. He was raised to the peerage as Lord Invernairn in 1921. See chapter: Ness Glen to Craigengillan;

Stanley Baldwin (1867 - 1947), three times Prime Minister, was also a visitor who enjoyed fishing and shooting at Craigengillan. See chapter: Ness Glen to Craigengillan;

Alexander Frederick McAdam of Craigengillan. He married Charlotte Tilke. He died in 1901 age 36, the estate passing to his wife;

Tom Walls (1883 – 1949), the former policeman and jockey was the driving force behind the Aldwych farces from about 1924. Most of these were successfully transferred to the screen with Walls as director and star. His first box office success was Rookery Nook (1930). His final film was the Interrupted Journey, completed in 1949 just before he died. He was a popular character actor, but his gambling kept him relatively poor. He was a leading racehorse owner and won the Epsom Derby in 1932 with 'April the Fifth.' He stayed at Craigengillan in 1931 for a week and enjoyed grouse shooting and fishing. He even advised Craigengillan staff that his horse would win the 1932 Derby.

CHAPTER 7
CRAIGENGILLAN - A VISION OF STEWARDSHIP

by Mark Gibson of Craigengillan

All the world is beautiful,
and it matters little where we go.
The spot where we chance to be
Always seems the best.

John Muir, 1890

"My dear chap, of course the water doesn't work, why do you think I sold the place"

"But it was working yesterday, have you any idea how to fix it?" I asked.

"Call a plumber," he answered gloomily, drawing deeply on a menthol cigarette.

"Are there any other problems with the house I should be aware of?"

"Well, when it rains, which is most of the time, the water cascades through the house."

"But its still very beautiful," I said, trying to be optimistic.

"Sneeze and it will fall down, it's a can of worms. The day you arrived and purchased Craigengillan was the luckiest day of my life," came the lugubrious reply. It was in fact the luckiest day of my life. On that inauspicious morning began my life at Craigengillan and Dalmellington and with it a trial, which would become a love affair.

Although I did not feel it then, that grey and smurry morning in late February, Craigengillan was in fact like Sleeping Beauty, a marvellous jewel waiting to be rediscovered. For close on a century she had gradually become disguised. As at the ancient temples of Cambodia, the jungle had temporarily reclaimed the Keeper's House, the Gardener's house, Find Me Out and the neighbouring cottage by the Glessel Burn. It was threatening the old mansion itself and advance armies of dry rot were devouring the timbers.

'Keep Out' signs heralded the two mile private approach and coiled barbed wire guarded house and bridges against invasion by persons unknown. Fences and dykes were largely horizontal, time honoured oaks hidden by dark spruce and rhododendrons and the sound of horses hoofs had long since last echoed in the cobbled yard. The stable clock was silent.

The Ordnance Gazetteer of 1903 describes Craigengillan. "Its mansion, on the left bank of the River Doon, $2^1/_2$ miles south by west of Dalmellington village, is a plain edifice, but has extensive grounds of great beauty, both natural and artificial. A waterfall, Dalcairnie Linn, on a neighbouring streamlet, makes a leap of more than 60 feet, and opens into a deep wooded dell. Berbeth [as Craigengillan was previously known] is the property of Alex Fred McAdam Esq.... [The landscape] rises into continuous eminences or mountain ridges...two [of the ridges] which flank the Doon at its egress from mountain-cradled Loch Doon, are rocky perpendicular elevations, and stand so close to each other for about a mile, as to seem cleft asunder by some powerful agency from above, or torn apart by some convulsive stroke from below. The

Craigengillan House from the Loch Doon Road. Over the years this house has seen many important visitors including foreign royals, British Prime Ministers and members of the aristocracy. See chapter: Loch Doon to Craigengillan.

Sir, o'er a gill I gat your card,
I trow it made me proud;
"See wha taks notice o' the bard!"
I lap and cried fu' loud.

Now deil-ma-care about their jaw,
The senseless, gawky million;
I'll cock my nose abune them a':
I'm roos'd by Craigen-Gillan!

'Twas noble, sir; 'twas like yourself',
To grant your high protection:
A great man's smile ye ken fu' well
Is aye a blest infection.

Tho', by his banes wha in a tub
Match'd Macedonian Sandy!
On my ain legs thro' dirt and dub,
I independent stand aye;

And when those legs to guid, warm kail,
Wi' welcome canna bear me,
A lee dyke-side, a sybow-tail,
An' barley-scone shall cheer me.

Heaven spare you lang to kiss the breath
O' mony flow'ry simmers!
An' bless your bonie lasses baith,
I'm tauld they're loosome kimmers!
An' God bless young Dunaskin's laird,
The blossom of our gentry,
An' may he wear and auld man's beard,
A credit to his country!

gorge between these heights, a narrow, lofty-faced pass, bears the name of Ness Glen, and opens at its north west extremity into the crescent-shaped plain."

Craigengillan includes several areas designated for their environmental, historic or architectural interest. The estate consists of some 3000 acres, encompassing a designed landscape, woodland, pasture and water, providing a wide diversity of habitat. There is evidence of ancient settlement from the final resting place by Bogton Loch of a local warlord who breathed his last on earth some four thousand years ago and from the medieval field boundaries and long houses shown up by the snow and by long evening shadows.

The recent history of Craigengillan, Berbeth as it was known, began with the granting of a Crown Charter to William McAdam in 1611, nearly four hundred years ago. From that time, the estate had never been sold until I came.

After keeping a low profile for more than a century after their involvement in the Raid of the Isles and their arrival at Craigengillan, the McAdams began to take an active interest in local affairs. By 1725 they were recorded as one of the foremost Ayrshire landowners. In a natural site in a wooded fold of the hills above the River Doon, there has long been a house at Craigengillan. In 1757 John McAdam took over from his father at Craigengillan. He was the great engineer and inventor of the family and with his kinsman John Loudon became a road and bridge builder and the inventor of tarmacadam. He became a popular figure in Dalmellington, providing employment and doing much good in the valley. A sturdy and able man with a vision much ahead of his time he was also a sponsor of the arts and an early encouragement to Robert Burns. Burns almost certainly stayed at Craigengillan and returned John's supper with a poem.

To Mr. McAdam, Of Craigengillan

In 1765 John McAdam re-designed the original house and added the first extension and the stables. He also built a substantial stone bridge over the river near the house and made the private approach road as a more direct way to Dalmellington. The road prior to this was from Straiton, along the road to Dalcairney Farm and over the hill to Craigengillan. In 1780 through his engineering skills he had devised a novel and excellent method of constructing dry stone dykes. In the process he had taught one of his key workers, John McKenzie, his new method of dry dyking. He granted a long-term lease of one of his properties to John McKenzie and set up a school of dry stone dyking at Craigengillan. Dykers came from all over to learn the McAdam method, which

proved to be the best in the country. It was at this time that fields were enclosed with granite dykes, many trees planted and extensive drainage undertaken. It was also at this time that Home Farmhouse, the Gatehouse and the first of the stone bridges crossing the River Doon was built, by French prisoners of war.

Adjacent to and possibly at one time linked to the house is a long tunnel, hewn out of the living rock and lined with stalactite encrusted dressed stone. Its original purpose is unknown. Although a branch leads in the direction of a deep underground vaulted chamber, conjectured to be an ice house, that use is by no means certain and the bloody experience of the Covenanters was still a fresh memory at the time it was built. In early Victorian times, probably 1840, the north east tower and crow stepped gables were added to the house and the observatory was constructed.

During the second half of the nineteenth century, Craigengillan was held by Alexander Frederick McAdam Cathcart. He was a generous man keen on sports and himself an excellent horseman, once racing the train to Ayr. With the arrival of the Dalmellington Iron Company at Dunaskin and the prospect of ironstone and coal mining he persuaded the farmers of the lower lying lands in the valley to change from sheep rearing to dairy farming. This way they would be

able to supply the new villages of Craigmark, Benquat, Pennyvennie and Beoch which were springing up, with their daily need of butter, milk and potatoes, etc. As well as a house in London to which they would entrain for the season with two coaches and a dozen horses at a cost of £66 (a groom at the time cost £15 per year), the McAdams had a holiday home on the Isle of Wight. On one of his visits there, he and some friends made an expedition to Dijon in France and there met a girl called Charlotte Tilke. They married, settled at Craigengillan and became involved in the life of the county.

The young married McAdams became notable socialite entertainers. From the years 1890 to 1900 an annual two-day event was also held in the Promised Land. The first day was a horse-riding gymkhana and on the second day an athletic sports meeting. Stands were erected for the viewing public; competitors came from far afield to compete. Dalmellington Band provided entertainment and the droothy palates of the bandsmen were quenched with ample refreshment. With Alexander McAdam's equestrian interests, breeding of horses became an industry at Craigengillan and these were trained and supplied to the British military. In 1899 a contingent of 40 of these horses saw service and were dispatched to South Africa to support Baden Powell's army during the Boer War and the Relief of Mafeking. Local vet Frederick Gavin took charge of these horses on their journey. He was the son of Alexander Gavin, General Manager of Dalmellington Iron Company. At the age of only 36 Alexander died and Charlotte took over the running of the house and estate. As a descendant described it 'her hair turned gold with grief' and she embarked upon a mammoth-spending spree. In the early 20th century the gardens were redesigned, a Japanese Water Garden created and Jansen, the foremost Parisian decorators, were commissioned to remodel the principal ground floor rooms of the mansion. Craigengillan is the only example in Scotland of their work and it is for this that the house is Listed Category A for its national architectural importance. Jansen continued in existence until the 1960's, one of their last commissions being the refurbishment of the White House for Jackie Kennedy.

The First War saw the building of the Bogton Airfield and School of Aerial Gunnery described elsewhere in this book. During the years of peace in Europe life returned to normal. Time and fortune did not stand still however and in 1919 large outlying parts of the estate were sold. The horses and carriages were gone from the stables and the groom replaced by a chauffeur who cared for the Rolls, a Daimler and a Renault shooting brake. Charlotte was succeeded by Alastair Gavin, nephew of Alexander and a London barrister.

Outside the boundaries of the estate the

Mr Pike with the Daimler car at Craigengillan

Mr Pike, chauffeur, with Mrs Charlotte McAdam's Rolls Royce at Craigengillan.

Leslie Pike was the son of the chauffeur at Craigengillan. This was taken about 1931 in the courtyard when he bought this De Dion Bouton car second hand for £10. It was a sight for locals to see a car, let alone own one. Leslie Pike is still alive in England aged 94.

world was changing. The deep coal mines closed, the hills were planted with coniferous forest and there were threats of nuclear dumping. The proud community admired by that famous Judge Lord Cockburn ('I wish I had Berbeth') was temporarily knocked back and unemployment reached terrible levels. The years passed and the ravages of time took their toll. From about 1900, almost nothing has been done to alter the designed landscape, apart from the creation of spruce plantations and limited planting of individual hardwoods. Many of the elements of the garden, including the hot houses and the temple-like gazebo on Corson's Knowe have been lost, and the Victorian gasworks and gasometer, the woodland cottages, the old brewery and the keeper's house have been allowed to crumble. The policy of benign neglect was not completely without compensation however; it applied equally to the management of the land. The result is an almost undisturbed range of woodland, wetland and other natural habitats, recognised for their importance by their designations as Site of Special Scientific Interest.

When I came to Craigengillan, every house was damp, cold and rotten, the fences and dykes were no longer stock proof and the farm was struggling. There was an atmosphere of anarchic gloom. I hoped to bring Craigengillan back to life. I wanted to manage it in an integrated way for the restoration and preservation of the main buildings and the designed landscape; for the long-term viability of the estate and its part in the wider community; for the welfare of the farmed

Fin'-Me-Oot' was the name of the house in the foreground. Behind is Glessel Cottage and to the right is the Gas Work building, all located near to Craigengillan House on the edge of the Glessel Burn. The two estate workers houses are being restored and should be completed in 2006.

animals; and for the conservation and enhancement of habitats and the wild flora and fauna which inhabit them.

The task before me was a daunting one but I believed in the future. On that first morning when the water had failed and the post brought only a pile of bills it was difficult to summon courage and to know where to start. I had inherited a fine shepherd in Willie Welsh and I asked him which job needed to be carried out most urgently. It turned out to be the replacement of a broken fence through which the lambs would escape into a dense plantation and then be unable to re-find their mothers. The job was done and the long fight back had begun.

The motto of the house is 'Steady, Calm'. It is a good one and I followed it. I had a long term vision, but having

found it I tried only to concentrate on what I needed to achieve for each month ahead. That way what was accomplished became more important than what was still to be done and my confidence grew. The farm is the lifeblood of Craigengillan and one of its main purposes. With healthy scepticism at first, Willie Welsh was persuaded to make the commitment necessary to achieve Organic Status for the land and its produce of lambs. So firm was that commitment that full conversion was confirmed within two years, the minimum possible. The land is now farmed much as it was by our forefathers, in harmony with the natural environment, and the organic lamb goes to supermarkets like Tesco and Sainsbury. The farm is now a viable unit and contributes to the place as a whole. No artificial fertilisers or sprays are used and the resulting explosion of wild flowers has been amazing. These in turn attract insects, which in turn support a remarkable diversity of birds.

The next task was to repair and restore all of the houses, starting with those lived in by people working here and followed by Craigengillan House and the stables. Many of the buildings are listed by Historic Scotland for their historical and architectural importance and all the restorations had to be carried out sympathetically and to a very high standard. We have had a terrific team, which has stayed together since building works began 40 months ago. In 2002 fifteen miles of new hedgerows were planted. Because the hedges need to be protected on both sides, a total of 30 miles

of new fencing had to be erected – a longer distance than from Dalmellington to Ayr and back. Weeded by hand to see the young trees beyond competition from grass and rushes, the hedges are now well on their way and the new fences make for much easier sheep management. In the years ahead the hedges will provide shelter for livestock and a hugely valuable wildlife habitat. They will also enhance the beauty of the place by binding together the different elements of a landscape which has already been formally recognised by Historic Scotland as being of national importance. At the same time as the hedges were being planted, several miles of John McAdam's eighteenth century stone dykes were being rebuilt, three new lochs created and the former Bogton Mine bing re-contoured and planted with trees.

Another very early priority was the creation of a well equipped office from which I could run my Chartered Surveying practice and deal with planning and administration of the estate. The part of the stables converted into a smoking room in 1900 was the obvious place and the lack of floor and ceiling quickly remedied. I discovered that so long as one had an oasis of order, however much of a building site the house was becoming, one could remain sane. To start with the house was somewhat gloomy and threatening. In the damp conditions the dry rot continued its slow and deadly advance and the position was critical. One Sunday as I was working in the garden a tremendous crash broke the afternoon stillness and a column of dust rose from the north wing.

It had finally and simply given up the ghost, fortunately with no consequent casualty.

While active restoration of the farm and the shepherd's house was taking place during my first year, I was getting to know and understand the house - essential if I was to learn to respect it and repair it without changing its character and atmosphere.

I was anxious too to ensure that the Gatehouse and Home Farm were dealt with; existence in both was then damp and depressing.

Having obtained consent from the planners and Historic Scotland for the restoration, I turned to the work itself. I knew that there was no point in putting out the project for formal tender, as there were simply too many unknowns. Instead I turned to Tommy Hiddleston, a master

builder from Dumfries whom I knew and trusted. We agreed a formula whereby he would work at cost and I would guarantee a management payment on top. In this way both our positions were protected. The arrangement worked so well that in the four years since Tommy and the team of local craftsmen working with him started work at Craigengillan, there has never been a single argument - almost unheard of in a project of this size and nature. Slowly, the tide of restoration moved from destruction – removal of rotten plaster and timbers and roofs, miles of acetylene gas lead pipes , windows and 1970's kitchen units. The roof was completely reslated and releaded, dormer windows and chimneys rebuilt, vaulted ceilings identical to the originals expertly constructed, painted panels restored and cornices, skirtings and architraves rerun. A magnificent heating system was installed, incorporating the fine old German

radiators fitted a century ago and still in mint condition.   Kilometres of electrical wiring were laid and the house was connected to mains water. As, chrysalis like, rooms re emerged the painters and decorators set to work with gallons of Farrow and Ball. Age stained panelling and floors were sanded and oiled. The house came back to life.

Probably the finest building at Craigengillan, the eighteenth century stable block was also crumbling and leaking. Listed Category A like the house for its national architectural importance, it clearly had to be restored. The question was - to what use should it be put? Most similar buildings on Scottish estates had been converted into flats, but this did not fit in with the philosophy of regeneration. The project was to be masterminded by Vicki Logan and we decided between us that the best use was the original use. We looked at the competition and realised that we could offer things that they could not. It would be possible for instance to ride from the stables not only along miles of beautiful estate tracks but also throughout the Galloway Forest, without touching a single tarmac road. The Georgian stables with their cobbled floors and wooden panelling arranged around a courtyard are of the highest architectural quality and nobody could ask for a finer home for their horse. Lastly, we would find the perfect, qualified person in Roslyn Fyfe to run the stables. Restoration of the old

buildings is now almost complete and we have built a stunning outdoor arena and a new general purpose storage building for haylage, straw and machinery.

A flat was created within the stables for Roslyn Fyfe, and the first horse arrived in summer 2004. In our business plan, we had forecast that the livery would be operating at 80% capacity within two years. The riding lessons took off quickly and it has been a joy to see the yard full of kids every day, not just riding but helping to muck out, groom, wash and feed. The farrier, too, is a regular visitor, shoeing the horses just as his forefathers would have done a hundred years ago. The livery side, after a slow start, suddenly surged ahead and by Easter 2005 we had 32 horses and were operating at full capacity. The business supports three jobs where before there were none.

Attracting visitors benefits not just the business but the village as well and I turned my mind to other ways to attract people here. In Victorian times, people had travelled from far and wide to walk the path through Ness Glen, described in contemporary guide books as the finest example in Britain of a true rock gorge, and even more poetically by the cartographer of the first edition of the Ordnance Survey in 1856 "A bold, round rocky hill, coated with deep brown moss, stands at the east entrance of the glen: immediately north of this the wood and precipice begin, consisting at first of a series of black shelving rocks, partially concealed by thick foliage. The cliff increases in height and rugged grandeur till, about midway, it reaches its greatest altitude in a long semicircular sweep. Steep as the wall of a house, it rises from the margin of the Doon to a height of nearly 300 feet. Thick old ivy is trellised all over the face of the impending steep; green lichens clinging to the rocks, uprooted trees hanging down into the abyss; upright firs and overhanging rocks are the other features of this tremendous wall. A belt of shady silver firs, which surmounts its jagged pinnacle, presents a fine contrast to the prevailing leaden colours of the stone. Beyond this the towering peaks and steep crags are repeated again and again, gradually softening away to a sloping wooded knoll. On the west side a winding walk has been carried up the bottom of the glen and another over the summit, terminating at the same point. There is a greater slope on this side, and the wild craggy features with which it abounds are much concealed by an old woven wood. A number of streamlets trickle through the fissures of the rock… and through these fissures are afforded the only glimpses to be had of the cliffs. The river side of the low walk is edged with a row of trees, many of the branches of which have been forced by the application of pressure during their early growth, to droop over the water. On the other side trails of ivy and shrubs of the evergreen class and rose-bushes have been trained up the rocks for some distance, and thus, by softening the ruggedness of that portion of the glen immediately under the eye of the visitor – affording him a means of contrast with the terrors overhead, whose sublime character might suffer from a close inspection – has been effected the only introduction of art which could in any way have heightened the effect of this imposing scenery."

At this time too, another guide book described Dalmellington as 'something of a mountain resort.' In the last half century the path had become all but impassable. Bridges had been lost, landslips blocked the way and huge trees had fallen across the water. The task of restoration was huge. Before we could do anything, we had to obtain consent and support from Scottish National Heritage as the Glen is a Site of Special Scientific Interest on account of its geology and the incredible diversity of mosses and ferns.

Work began in the summer of 2004 with the construction of a new suspension bridge across the Doon and the re-creation of the path following the top of the gorge. In 2005 we began and completed the mile and a half of path following the water's edge, past rapids, waterfalls and vertical moss covered cliffs. It was impossible to bring machinery into the gorge, so a team was assembled from Dalmellington to undertake the task by hand. The path was formed with pickaxe and shovel, blood and sweat but luckily no tears. Twenty one bridges were built to span otherwise impassable chasms, each one carried by hand. Finally, some eighty tonnes of stone were wheel barrowed in for the final surface. Already the path is attracting new visitors as word spreads and canoeists have come from all over Scotland to test their white water skills.

The stables and the Ness Glen path have proved that a regeneration of the Doon Valley based on tourism is a sustainable reality and other big projects are at an advanced stage. A further footpath is planned through Dalcairney Gorge and its famous falls and onward to the summit of Auchenroy Hill through a newly established 250 acre native woodland. From the summit, there are amazing views into the Galloway Forest, the Merrick and across the sea to Ailsa Craig and Arran.

Straiton has already established itself as a walking centre, generating over £2 million a year for the local economy. The spectacular new walks in Dalmellington will attract even more and make this part of Scotland known as a top destination for walkers.

Two further projects have received planning consent - a state of the art Outdoor Activity and Environmental Centre to be developed on the shore of Bogton Loch and a refrigerated Outdoor Curling Centre, the first of its kind in Europe, adjacent to the site of the Victorian curling pond on the estate.

These projects will create many jobs and bring a substantial number of visitors to Dalmellington. Both will require tremendous effort, commitment and cash. Because visitors will be attracted as much to the beauty of the surroundings as to the facilities themselves, neither project can proceed until the dark threat of wind turbine developments is lifted. The prospects for these developments have united the community in opposition and attracted record numbers of individual objections. Hopefully reason will prevail and the Doon Valley will be allowed to conquer the legacy of the past and create a bright new future.

The spirit of Burns is alive and strong and it is the combination of this spirited Dalmellington community, the natural wonders of the landscape and the projects themselves which will ensure success.

From scenes like these Old Scotia's grandeur springs,
That makes her loved at home, revered abroad:
Princes and Lords are but the breath of kings,
'An honest man's the noblest work of God.'

The Cotter's Saturday Night
Robert Burns

CHAPTER 8
DALMELLINGTON

Guarded by many a grand old hill,
And many a diamond-sparkling rill,
Where River Doon, at her sweet will,
Flows gently on,
I see thee nestling calm and still,
Dalmellington

There's bold Ben Beoch's rugged scaur,
And those great hills that stretch afar
Towards the steep cliffs of 'The Star,'
Where I would climb,
And muse on days of bloody war
Mid scenes sublime.

Dalmellington
Matthew Anderson
(The policeman poet of the Ayrshire Constabulary)

The upper section of the Doon valley is an intriguing area with a fascinating industrial and social history stretching far back on the wings of time. In *Pigot's Directory* of 1837 an interesting insight into the life of the village is given. "A Burgh of Barony, this thriving little place is pleasantly situated on the north bank of the water of Doon. The manufacture of blankets, carpets, plaiding, and the weaving of cotton goods, together with the coal mines in the neighbourhood, afford employment to many in the industrious class. These mines are at present leased to Mr William Sloss, of the Cross Keys, a very popular Inn here."

The village lies at a height of 600 feet above sea level some 15 miles south east of Ayr and is situated about 1 mile east of the romantic River Doon, made famous by the world-renowned bard, Robert Burns, who certainly knew this welcoming corner of Ayrshire. The origins of the village name can be read in two ways, either as Dal Muilean Tuin, "the fort on the plain of the mills," or Dal Meallan Tuin, "the fort on the plain of the hills." There is evidence for both as there are mills, and there are hills, or mounds, notably the famous Mote located at the east end of the village, a large smooth eminence proudly rising above the town, where the ancient Pictish inhabitants perhaps met to settle matters of law and custom. At such places matters of concern to all were raised, or "mooted," for discussion.

The visitor would benefit from taking time to explore the village and surrounding area. The old cemetery is in a shameful condition having been extensively vandalised over the years and many historic headstones have been lost. However, it contains a Covenanting memorial and a plaque to the blacksmith poet of the village, Robert Hetrick (1769 – 1849). The Dalmellington Parish Church (1846) and the former Lamloch Church (1851) are notable buildings. The village museum at Cathcartston will also reveal much of the history of the area including information about the weaving and mining industries. This homely museum mounts regular displays reflecting the life and times of the village. Those with time to spare would enjoy a walk to the Pickans Dyke, located above the current cemetery or to the dramatic waterfall at Dalcairnie. Ben Beoch Craig, a miniature Giants Causeway, dominates the road to Cumnock, about 2 miles outside the village, and is well worth the extra effort of a strenuous hillwalk.

The Muck (Moik) water streams through the centre of the village and on many occasions, particularly 1926 and 1934, the centre of the village has been devastated by severe floods vividy remembered by a diminishing number of the oldest residents.

According to William Douglas (*In Ayrshire - 1872*) the history of Dalmellington can be traced as far back

The Dalmellington Coat of Arms highlighting the town's association with brass banding, fishing, mining and forestry.

as 1003 when there was some shape of existence at its present location. Mention is also made of the little church in Dalmellington in the records of the Diocese of Glasgow towards the end of the 13th century. It is known that this ancient church was situated in the old graveyard below the mote in the village. No trace of this church exists today.

Dalmellington was strategically located on an ancient routeway from the south which linked up with the Old Edinburgh Road to Galloway and the Pilgrim Way to Whithorn. This left the village caught between a strong royalist presence at Carsphairn and a very active Covenanting one in Cumnock.

Woodrow asserts that 600 troops, armed with cannon, ammunition, iron shackles and fetters, were quartered in the parish in 1685, living off the land and causing considerable upset to the local population which then numbered only a few hundred, on whom the soldiers would have been billeted. Fines were levied for worship in the open air, people were imprisoned, families dispersed and houses plundered all because local men stood out against Episcopacy. Quintin Dick, an elder in the parish church, said to have been a wise, well educated and caring man, suffered terribly during these years. He was imprisoned in 1684 and a year later he was taken from Edinburgh to be detained in Dunottar Castle. He would have been deported, but was left behind because it was believed he was dying. He recovered and returned to Dalmellington where he endeavoured to heal the differences which had separated the Presbyterian brethren of the parish. Another elder of the parish church, Roger Dunne of Benquat was on his way home from Carsphairn Fair when he was ambushed and killed by some rogues. His grave can be seen in Carsphairn Kirkyard. Many other young men, especially those from the farming community, became involved with the Covenanters and the names of Sloss, McAdam, McWhirter and Paterson appear in the Covenanting records. Dalmellington Parish Church (1846), formerly known as the Kirk o' the Covenant until 1983, has a very valuable collection of Covenanting silver. The small cups dating from 1637 and 1650 are reputed to have been taken by Rev Alexander Stevenstone (Parish Minister 1648 -1680) who adhered to the

Covenanting ways, into the nearby basaltic pillars at Benbeoch Craig (1,522') where they were used to give communion. They are still used today at communion services and remain an important link with the past. The current parish minister is Reverend Kenneth Yorke and he oversaw the linkage with Patna Church in 2004. The session clerk is Miss Anna McHattie.

Like many other Ayrshire towns of the 17th and 18th century, hand-loom weaving was one of the stable cottage industries, but as the 19th century progressed this trade went into a long and gradual decline, to be replaced by the growth of the mining industry with which the Doon Valley villages are proudly associated. From the late 1840's The Dalmellington Iron Company (founded 1848) and its successors operated dozens of pits and drift mines in the Doon Valley extracting coal and ironstone and names such as Bowhill, Polnessan, Dalharco, Houldsworth, Jellieston, Burnfoot, Drumgrange, Dunaskin, Corbie Craigs, Craigmark, Minnivey, Bogton, Sillyhole, Chalmerston, Pennyvenie, Clawfin, Benbain and Beoch all had many underground workings until deep mining ceased in 1978 with the closure of Pennyvenie. A special era in the history of the Doon Valley had come to an end and within a further two decades all deep mining in Scotland met a similar fate. However, open cast mining was to become a huge industry in terms of coal extracted, but unfortunately it employed very few workers.

The records of the Dalmellington Iron

Dalmellington Primary School
Qualifying Class 1956
Back row (l to r): George Orr,
Jim Halbert, Ian Calderwood,
Ian McConnochie, Neil Chambers,
David Clark, John Murphy, Val Pirrie
and Billy Brown.
Middle row: Henry Stirrat,
David Barclay, Jim Campbell,
Alan Porter, Charles Paterson,
Billy McLauchlan, Billy Gemmell,
Matthew Park, David Brown,
Miss Forbes (Canadian Teacher who was
on exchange).
Front row: Nancy Hamilton, Betty Boyd,
Dorothy Tyson, Helen Feelie, Ilda Given,
Sandra Gault, Ann Salmond,
Sandra McCulloch, Sheila Woodcock,
Elizabeth Murray and Jeanette Rowan.
(On ground): Sandra Orr and
Marlene Clydesdale.

Company and its successor, Bairds and Dalmellington show a total of 43 pits in the area from 1845 until the present day when all that remains is extensive open-cast mining to the east of and overlooking the village. Incredibly many thousands of tons of coal are extracted by this method and between two and four trains per day with up to forty wagons on each transport this mountain of coal from Chalmerston loading point.

The village is proud to be able to boast one of the finest brass bands in the United Kingdom. Dalmellington Band was formed in 1864. For many folk, when the name Dalmellington is mentioned, they will immediately tell you about the band. In short the town is synonymous with its outstanding brass band. Under the baton of Hugh Johnstone MBE, who has served the band from his boyhood days, they won the Scottish championships in 1969 and 1976. In 1978 under the baton of guest conductor, Richard Evans, they were again Scotland's premier band. A special recent highlight was the celebration of the Diamond Jubilee Cecil Oughton Memorial Slow Melody Contest which took place in Dalmellington Community Centre on 9th April, 2005. The adjudicator was Bruce Fraser and the prizes were presented by Miss Anne Joss and Miss Peggy McQueen. The contest was won by Derick Kirkwood, acknowledged to be one of Scotland's top trombone players. Interestingly, the first Slow Melody in 1947 was also won by a trombone player, Robert Hill, who was a life-long servant to the band and local community.

2005 will also see the completion of a new band hall, located in the grounds of Dalmellington Community Centre. This purpose built hall will allow the band to develop the skills of existing players and introduce young players to the world of brass banding. The dedicated band committee have built up a strong following of committed patrons whose support has been invaluable over recent years. The current conductor of the band is Archie Hutchison, with his own roots firmly in Dalmellington he was a member of the band from age 10. The band president is also a life-long player, Bert Ritchie, who has been a driving force in achieving funding for the new band hall. Perhaps the secret of the success of this dynamic village band is first class team work and a willingness by players, committee members, patrons and villagers in general to support the band with its long and precious tradition of producing wonderful music in an atmosphere of fun and friendship.

In many ways the band has provided a

degree of continuity within the local community and the villagers are rightly proud of the tradition of outstanding music and service provided by their men of brass. Having the opportunity to listen to the band in concert or on the competitive stage makes one proud of the long tradition of brass banding in the village. Indeed, for a little village like Dalmellington to have sustained a flourishing top-class brass band since 1864 is truly remarkable. Long may this tradition continue. Arthur W Wilson could have been thinking and speaking about the band and its traditions when he wrote these poignant words in the Dalmellington High School song, "May the Sons of our Sons Remember, Dalmellington with Pride." Long may the band continue to be, for many, the proud public face of Dalmellington.

The Dalmellington Curling Club is of even earlier vintage, having been established in the village in 1841 and like the band, still going strong today. Founded in the Black Bull Inn, Dalmellington, on 3 December,1841. It was re-named Dalmellington Craigengillan Curling Club in 1881, in recognition of the help and assistance given to the club by its patron, the Hon. J McAdam Cathcart of Craigengillan. The first rink was built by the patron for the use of club members at Miekle Loup on the approach road to the estate in September 1849 and used till 1887 when the exit level of Bogton Loch was raised. A new pond was constructed at a cost of £62.2.6d at the Tile Works north of the Manse Burn in Dalmellington and this was in use till the opening of Ayr Ice Rink in 1943. The oldest trophy is the Colonels Gold Medal, presented to the club in 1854. This trophy was to be played for between Dalmellington and the adjoining parishes and it was last played for in 1971. Due to a dispute no game has been played since then. The club celebrated its 150th anniversary with a large garden party at Craigengillan House on 26 May 1991 when Dalmellington Band entertained a large company of Ayrshire Curlers. This was followed by a dinner dance. The Patron was Mr Alastair B Gavin at that time owner of Craigengillan and the president was John Collins of Dalmellington. The toast to Dalmellington Craigengillan Curling Club was delivered by Sheriff David B Smith. The Master of Ceremonies was club secretary, Kennedy Ferguson. This was a truly historic occasion for the oldest club in Dalmellington. Interestingly, Robert Hetrick, the local poet was also a keen curler and wrote this poem as a tribute to the roaring game.

White winter on ilk hill and plain,
Is a' its powers unfurling,
And giving Scotia's sons again,
Their favourite game of curling;
That game which is like nature free,
The Caledonia's darling;
For ever cursed let him be,
Wha'd tax the game o' curling.

On ilka river, loch and pond,
The bonspiel is contested;
And, though their hearts are warm and keen,
Yet envy is resisted;
For, when the game is at an end,
And the glasses round are whirling,
Then ilka ane drinks to his friend,
And the glorious game of curling.

White Winter On Ilka Hill
Robert Hetrick, Dalmellington 1826

Similarly, St. Thomas (Kilwinning) Dalmellington lodge of freemasons was formed in 1864, again highlighting that Dalmellington has a long tradition of organisations to meet the social needs of local people. The Church of Scotland Guild, Scouts, BBs and local football teams provide yet more opportunities for local people to enjoy social networking.

Coal mining, from the 1830s until 1978,

Jan Murray and her father Tom (93). Both great supporters of Dalmellington Band.
Tom is the father of Archie Hutchison, conductor of Dalmellington Band.
Photo taken at the 50th Cecil Oughton Memorial Slow Melody in Dalmellington Community Centre in 2005.

was the major employer of Doon Valley men and during the writer's boyhood days the working pits connected with Dalmellington were Beoch, Pennyvenie, Minnivey, Bogton and Chalmerston. Between 1951 when the writer was born and 1978, all these pits had ceased working. Indeed by 2002 there was no working deep mine in the whole of Scotland, which clearly demonstrates that an entire industry can literally disappear in forty years. Remarkable by any standard that can be applied. There is also a danger that the mining tradition can quickly be forgotten before its history is recorded.

Indeed the pace of change and the fact that the past is not automatically remembered was recently highlighted during a conversation about coal mining when one young school boy quizzically replied to a question on coal mining, "What's coal?" The age-old battle between continuity and change means that what was accepted by one generation can be totally alien to the next. Generations of hard working and very proud Doon Valley men grafted in the pits, often at great cost in lives lost, injuries sustained and broken health due to intolerable working conditions. It is important that our social

and industrial heritage is remembered by future generations.

Indeed it was common in earlier times for family groupings to work together as a team in the pits and this was the case in respect of both the writers own grandfathers, Hugh 'Fergie' Hose and Tommy Reid, who worked in local mines with their own sons. Mining is no more in Dalmellington nor indeed in Scotland. But hopefully those who had family connections with the industry will be justly proud of their mining heritage and will tell those who come after them of the hard-won coal and the proud men who were miners.

Wi plenty o sic trees, I trow,
The warld would live in peace, man;
The sword would help to mak a plough,
The din o war wad cease, man.
Like brethren in a common cause,
We'd on each other smile, man;
And equal rights and equal laws
Wad gladden every isle, man.

The Tree of Liberty
Robert Burns

Dalmellington folk are rightly proud of their rich social and industrial past. The village, however, lacks any local employment of significance. But it has licensed premises in abundance. There is the Eglinton Hotel, the Dalmellington Inn, The Blackbull, The Doon Tavern, The Snug Bar, Dalmellington Bowling Club and the 433 Masons Club. Meanwhile, in Burnton there is the Craigmark Inn and in Bellsbank the Louden Tavern, formerly called the

Merrick Inn. Dalmellington is reasonably well served with general shops, a branch of the Royal Bank of Scotland, post office, baker, several newsagents, chemist, florist, two cafes, a first class community centre and Ayr Road Petrol Station which doubles as a small general shop.

The village was given a great boost on 10 September 2001 when the Dalmellington Area Centre was officially opened by the Princess Royal. The motto of the centre is "Progress through Partnership." The multi-purpose building brings together several departments of East Ayrshire Council, Strathclyde Police, the Health Centre and a Business

Technology and Training Centre in what was a first of its kind in Scotland, highlighting the importance of partnership working. Moreover, on 10 February 2002, Andy Kerr MSP, Minister for Finance and Public Services in the Scottish Executive, planted a tree in the grounds of the area centre to mark the centre winning an Office in Public Management Award for its innovative service to the community. The local Member of Parliament until the general election on 12 May 2005, Rt Hon George Foulkes, was subsequently elevated to the House of Lords taking the title, Lord Foulkes of Cumnock. The current Member of Parliament is Sandra Osborne. The member of the Scottish

William and Mary Johnstone of 59 Burnton celebrate their golden wedding celebration in February 1955 with a party in the old Masonic Hall. Older folk will identify a large number of well known folk from Dalmellington area.

Parliament and Justice Minister is Cathy Jamieson. The Doon Valley Councillors are Elaine Stewart and Elaine Dinwoodie. All are members of the Scottish Labour Party.

Most people travel to Ayr or further afield to find work. Attracting tourists has been helped with the creation of the Scottish Industrial Railway Centre at Minnivey where some excellent

Looking towards Benbeoch Craig with the St Barbara's Church which was demolished in 2002 after lying abandoned and vandalised for several years.

locomotives have been preserved. A forthcoming change which will add greatly to the Dunaskin Experience is the intention to move all rolling stock from Minnivey to Waterside which, hopefully, will attract many more tourists to this fine museum site. However, attracting a large employer of local labour is undoubtedly the greatest need to help regenerate an area of historical significance and outstanding natural beauty. Sadly, the Booktown project proved to be a failure, the small number of dealers having left the old High School building by the end of 2004. Radio Scotland also gave the town a welcome boost in 2004 when Dalmellington was the scene for regular live radio broadcasts and this helped to showcase the village to the rest of Scotland for a period of 12 months. This project involved the pupils and staff of Doon Academy as well as local people in the community who were regularly on the air broadcasting their views on a whole range of topical subjects.

Finally, Dalmellington, like the rest of the Doon valley is still very much a friendly close-knit community, albeit many of the real characters, most miners, of early days are no longer with us. Those who have left Dalmellington hold it in high regard and enjoy sojourns back to places which are so inextricably linked with boyhood days - love of home and parents, love of happy care-free childhood days and love of friends. These are some of the most enduring sentiments of the human heart and this nostalgia for the days that have gone, persist wherever we go, and however high we may climb.

We twa hae run aboot the braes,
And pou'd the gowans fine,
But we've wander'd monie a weary fit
Sin' auld lang syne.

We twa hae paidl'd in the burn
Frae morning sun till dine,
But seas between us braid hae roar'd,
Sin Auld Lang Syne.

All of us still yearn for the scenes of our childhood and doubtless often think of loved ones from whom we are separated in life and death. Who, dear reader, can have anything but a twinkling gleam in the eye as we float back on the wings of time to our childhood days and think of our parents and friends. The exile, far across the seas, still hears the curlew calling in the hills of home. Such is the nostalgia which all of us feel for our home and folk of yesteryear who played such an important part in shaping our lives. Think of happy days at Pirkelly Burn, Loch Doon, Craigengillan Estate, fishing on the Doon, watching good old Craigmark, guddling for trout in the Muck burn, working in the pits, or taking a jaunt down to Ayr by bus or on the fondly remembered steam trains of the Dalmellington Branch line. Recall the characters of the town of your day. Above all, be proud that you and yours were part of the Dalmellington and Doon Valley story.

Since I dwelt here long years have fled,
And many a flower its bloom has shed,
And many a lovely lass has wed
Her darling one,
Who now in thee lies cold and dead,
Dalmellington

Alas! My dear old native home;
Apart from thee my footsteps roam,
But back with heavy heart I come
This solemn day
To lay a comrade in the tomb,
Then turn away.

Verses suggested at the funeral of Constable John Craig, at Dalmellington, on March 24, 1910

Matthew Anderson
The Policeman-poet of the Ayrshire Constabulary

CHAPTER 9

CECIL OUGHTON - MUSICAL MAESTRO

Hugh Johnstone MBE of Dalmellington Band provided much of the material in this short chapter.

Cecil Oughton was the youngest son of William and Violetta Oughton and was born on 6th February, 1923 at 27 William Street, Hetton-le-hole. Along with his two brothers Cecil was brought to their new home at Dalmellington in 1927 when William Oughton took up a post as conductor of Dalmellington Band. Cecil's formative years were spent at Dalmellington High School. When age 7 he was introduced to the cornet by his father and his natural ability was such that he was soon playing duets with his brother, Robert, who also went on to become a top cornet player and conductor. As he began to mature as a player it soon became evident to fellow bandsman that Cecil was destined to be a player of distinction. However, he went through a period of rebellion and he began to drift away from brass band music and brass bands, to the great disappointment of his father. This proved to be a source of great friction within the Oughton family.

Cecil, however, did not drift away from the world of music altogether. His tastes had developed and he was a lover of jazz music and the Big Band scene. As the arguments continued to dominate family life, at the age of 14 years, Cecil left home without his father knowing until he was discovered missing.

Cecil found himself in Morecombe,

Lancashire and the chance sighting of an advertisement for a young trumpet player was to change his musical life for ever. The advertisement was for Nat Gonella's new Georgian's Dance Band. A successful audition followed and a new life began for this talented brass instrumentalist.

In those early days Cecil was looked after by Nat Gonella's wife, Stella Moya, who sang with the band. After much persuading, he eventually told them where he came from. Shortly after that he made contact with his father who immediately travelled from Dalmellington to Morecambe to try and persuade his son to come back home. However, despite the pleas of his concerned father, Cecil had made up his mind. He knew exactly what he wanted to do and that was to stay and play with the Big Band. Nat Gonella realised that he had a prestigious talent on his hands and reassured William Oughton that if he allowed his son to remain with the band, both he and his wife would look after him as if he was his own son. William agreed that under those terms his son could stay and pursue his dream career.

By 1939 the rift between father and son had been healed, so much so that Cecil invited his father to Blackpool to watch one of the band's performances. You can

A new hall for Dalmellington Band is beginning to take shape in January 2005. This is located in the grounds of Dalmellington Community Centre.

Had we never lov'd sae kindly,
Had we never lov'd sae blindly,
Never met – or never parted –
We had ne'er been broken hearted.

Ae Fond Kiss
Robert Burns

Cecil Oughton was the youngest son of William Matthew Oughton, the bandmaster of Dalmellington band from 1926 until 1959. He was an excellent cornet player and went on to play with the Nat Ganella Band.

Robert Oughton, was the second oldest son of William Matthew Oughton, bandmaster at Dalmellington from 1926 until 1959 when Hugh Johnstone took over the baton. Robert came to Dalmellington with his father in 1926 and was educated at Dalmellington Higher Grade School and learned cornet with Dalmellington Band. Such was his ability that age 15 he joined the famous Munn and Felton band as assistant principal cornet to the great Elgar Clayton. Age 17 he joined Grimethorpe Colliery band as principal cornet and was at that time the highest paid cornet player in the country. In 1940 he joined the Scots Guards and on being demobbed in 1947 was appointed principal cornet with Ransome & Marles Band. A noted adjudicator and conductor, he died aged 75 in July 1995 and was buried in Dalmellington cemetery alongside his father. He was regarded as one of the finest players of his era.

Dalmellington Band was formed in 1864. The current players were snapped in May 2005 at a concert in Dalmellington Community Centre.
Back row (l to r): Alison Roseblade, Leah Murdoch, Elaine Roxburgh, Lindsay Roxburgh, Eric McFadzean, David Roxburgh, Stephen Reid, Sandy McAughtrie and Diane Logan.
Middle row: Derick Kirwood, Carrie Bell, John Boax, David McLean, Jane Baillie, Chris Dale, Calum McPhail, Allison O'Donnell and John Calderwood
Front row: Brian Mackie, Brian Keast, Billy Whalen, Bert Richie (band president), Archie Hutchison (conductor), David McKellar, Ian Taylor, George Hoffin and Sandy McCulloch.

imagine what William thought when he discovered that Cecil was being paid £24 per week, equivalent to £796 today, a wage that William could only have dreamt of in those days. Cecil and the band played at each venue Monday through to Saturday and then travelled on Sunday to the next venue. It was a very busy schedule for a mere teenager, but his playing ability on jazz trumpet was recognised as being exceptional.

In 1942 Cecil was called up for compulsory national service in the Royal Artillery. On 2 July, 1944 his parents received official notification that Cecil had been killed in action. At the time of his death 21 year old gunner Cecil Oughton was a member of the 59th Royal Artillery Tank Regiment. Cecil was buried at Benneyville-la-Campagne War Cemetery along with over 2,000 other Commonwealth burials of the Second World War, 140 of them were unidentified and five were Polish graves.

The name of Cecil Oughton lives on today in Dalmellington in the form of two awards. One is a music trophy awarded annually at Doon Academy, which replaced the former Dalmellington High School. The second is the Dalmellington Band's own Cecil Oughton Memorial Slow Melody contest which celebrated its Diamond Jubilee in 2005 with the winner being Derick Kirkwood, a popular member of the band and one of Scotland's finest exponents of the trombone.

The memory of Cecil Oughton and his interesting story will long remain fresh in Dalmellington as an example of a headstrong but exceptionally talented musician who made the ultimate sacrifice for his country.

The trumpets sound, the banners fly,
The glittering spears are ranked ready,
The shouts o' war are heard afar,
The battle closes deep and bloody.

The Silver Tassie
Robert Burns

CHAPTER 10
WATERSIDE REVISITED

by Alice Robertson

Alice Robertson, raised at Waterside and now living in Edinburgh, is the grand-daughter of popular Waterside minister, Rev R D Potter, the last minister to serve in what was by then a dwindling rural community. Her happy childhood days were spent in Waterside. Readers will enjoy travelling with Alice on a journey down memory lane to revisit the Waterside of Alice's early years. The names and events she recalls will doubtless strike a chord with many former villagers.

I have revisited Waterside a number of times over the years since leaving Patna for Edinburgh in 1962 and it always feels strange approaching the village from the museum or works direction. It is almost like reliving memory back to front! When I first arrived, with my family, in 1956, we came by train and walked up the brae and over the railway bridge to Clover Park. This was the route we always took for buses and trains. The last time I was there, in June 2002, I needed to find a route from the works that led me back to the beginning of my association with the village and a logical structure or framework for both the recall of and the recording of memories. I am grateful to John Moore and John Dinwoodie for helping me with names and other information but a fuller account would require contact with more people that I had been familiar with.

We had come, in 1956, to join my grandfather the Rev. R D Potter who had been the minister of Waterside and Lethanhill since 1953. Apart from two years in Petrievie and three years in Singapore on RAF camps, I lived mostly with him until I left home at the age of nineteen. When we returned from Singapore to the UK the alternative was a transit camp, for an indefinite period, and my parents wanted our education to continue in Scotland. Grandpa was, at that time, living at the end of Clover Park in a cottage consisting of a living room, bedroom, kitchen and outside lavatory. On the site of this cottage there is now a large boulder sitting under a small tree. The boulder is a memorial to John Boyd, a Waterside resident, who was brutally murdered in his own kitchen.

After two hours on the road from Edinburgh it was about lunchtime when John, my husband, and I arrived so our first stop was *The Chimney's Restaurant* where we enjoyed a pleasant lunch. Afterwards we headed up towards the glen, a place often visited, alone, with friends or with family during the time I lived in Waterside. The works area seems strangely ghostly and quiet now without the smells of the brick kilns; the puffing

I remember the 'exiles':
they came north with the sun.
You could pick them out easily
by their impressiveness:
birds of passage, with distinctive plumage
and a new note in their throats.

Their spouses lingered
on the edges of conversations;
their children spoke in tutored tongues
and played cricket endlessly
across bogs.

Now I have a city child
I bring him north.
He is the one apart,
with awkward smiles.

De Luca, Christine (1995): *Voes and Sounds* Shetland Library Lerwick p20

of pugs; the clanking of bogies; and men working, whistling, laughing, joking and singing. The brickworks were still in operation during that time and we would pass men working, drinking tea or eating their pieces. There was always time for a friendly crack or two with any passers by. Every time I go back I find evidence of things I did not know about the village at that time. For example, on a previous visit, we discovered that there had been rows of cottages inside the works area. Young trees, bushes and wild flowers now cover the foundations of these.

It was a gloriously warm, sunny and pleasant day with many beautiful wild flowers in bloom: briar rose, wild orchids, ragged robin, white campion, hog weed, wild strawberries, buttercups, vetch, and clover, to name a few. The area is an impressive wild life sanctuary. We walked as far as we could along the glen but I was disappointed, as on previous occasions, not to be able to go beyond the beginning of the aquaduct. The duct part is full of stagnant water and wild plants, and the wooden path has entirely disintegrated. This was a walk often taken to the top of the glen and beyond with my mother and family or alone. On another occasion we may have time to venture down beside the burn or walk along the top of the glen. Returning in the direction of Ardoon House we passed the reservoir now wonderfully overgrown with trees, bushes and other wild plants. It is difficult to make out the sides now and it has become a haven for wild life of all kinds.

Ardoon House and its gardens were unfamiliar territory when occupied but I would often hear the sounds of the house with people and cars coming and going while gathering kindling for the fire in the woods. It seemed full of life and it has been sad, on previous visits, to find this house, in such a beautiful setting, looking so derelict. There were signs now that it is being restored: the roof had been retiled and there were new beams between the floors. The Ardoon woods used to be particularly lovely in the spring when the daffodils and then the wild hyacinths were in bloom. During a previous visit I had noticed badger sets.

Leaving the house we continued in the direction of the top railway line behind the Greenhill and Barley Park rows. Although this is a very beautiful walk the sounds of pugs, bogies and men were missing here too. There are far more wild flowers here than before and the gardens of the rows, which sloped down from the track, have turned into a small, dense, wood. Grandpa used to walk along here with his suitcase gathering any coal that had fallen off the trucks. He used to say, along with his infectious giggle, that if anyone saw him with a suitcase they would just think he was carrying his robes! We walked as far as the steps down towards what had been the gap between the Clover Park and Barley Park rows. Twice, further along and before flitting to Patna, I walked with Grandpa up the incline to Lethanhill to remembrance services around the war memorial with tea afterwards in the surviving former Miners Institute.

On many a beautiful day, and in other kinds of weather, I sat on these steps or the Green Hill behind watching and listening to the sounds of the village, and enjoying the view across the valley. This view is enhanced now by the lower height of the slag bing and it is possible to see many previously hidden features on the opposite side of the valley - but somehow I miss this heap. In its larger form it had a strange foreboding and awesome attraction of its own. I would wonder about the origin of this slag in the deep tunnels and cavities of the earth and if, through time, the resulting empty spaces might change the configuration of the earth. This bing seemed a large, conspicuous and fitting memorial to the many men who produced it, particularly those who were maimed or killed in the attempt and those who died from lung and heart related conditions due to long hours underground.

It was here in Clover Park, February 1956 that our familiarity with Waterside began. We may not have experienced the village in its heyday but we were privileged to experience a little of what life might have been like. Somehow we all fitted into this little cottage (I know much larger families than ours had fitted into cottages like this in the past). It did not seem overcrowded at the time but I was always an outdoor child spending little time inside. There were some advantages, not least the fact that it was always warm inside between the stove in the scullery and the living room fire. These heated the whole cottage and there was electricity from the works. We had just returned from the tropics and were not yet acclimatized. Much of my

previous childhood had been spent in manses during the years of rationing where for good reason most of the day was spent in the warm kitchen. Sitting room fires would only be lit in the evenings, on special occasions, or for visitors. There was no heating in the bedrooms upstairs. In Shetland coal was a precious commodity not only because of rationing but because it had to arrive by sea. With no electricity we relied on Tilley and other oil lamps, as well as torches for light. Here there was no bathroom and only an outside lavatory but again in cold manses we were used to receptacles that went under beds and bathing in a tub in front of the kitchen fire. In Shetland it was often far too cold to bathe in the bathroom built onto the back of the house. Life was, perhaps, most difficult for my mother as washing was mostly done in an outside brick boiler in all weathers. Drinking water had to be collected from a spring outside the back door and the fire and stove had to be cleaned out daily and regularly fed coal.

There was running water in the house but that was unsuitable for drinking. The spring, or sheuch as it was known, was just outside our lavatory and a meeting place for the women still resident in Clover Park. It could be entertaining just to sit inside and listen to their gossip as well as the voices of children playing. There was still quite a feeling of community and often on nice evenings the residents would sit outside on their front doorsteps, or wander up and down the row chatting, joking and laughing. Children would be playing all around in all weathers. This was my first and last

experience of shawlie women: women who carried their babies in shawls wrapped round themselves and their babies. My mother quickly became friends with the other women, in particular, May Brown. May was a generous and good friend to many, especially during the time of relocation from Waterside to Patna. The women

Drumgrange Incline runs from the north side of Waterside and rises steeply to the Drumhead near to Lethanhill. It was laid down about 1865 and is unlikely to have operated after 1930. It was used for transporting coal and other goods from the valley to the plateau above.

spent many a Thursday evening together even after moving to Patna. My mother used to read their cups but took fright when things foretold seemed to begin to come true! Another good family friend was Mrs Flora Scott who lived in Hillend

South and taught in Patna. Our garden, stretching up towards the railway line and now full of wild things was a useful source of food. Grandpa always grew potatoes and other vegetables wherever he stayed. There was nothing he liked more that a boiled fresh potato, onion and other vegetable with a chunk of cheese for supper – even after an evening

Four teachers at Waterside Primary School when it closed in 1958. It later opened as the St Xaviers for Catholic children and continues to this day. (l to r): Miss Anne Joss, F Scott, Mrs Ross and Mr Robert Taylor (headmaster). Behind are the rows in Barley Park.

visiting and innumerable cups of tea (or whatever), scones and cakes.

Almost immediately I became friendly with Janette Guthrie who visited her aunt next door at weekends. Miss Guthrie had a magnificent collection of colourful luxurious rag rugs that seemed to cover every floor in the cottage. One could only wonder at the lifetime of clothes and soft furnishings, as well as the memories of the people who owned them, woven into these. Janette used to stay with her aunt at weekends and introduced me to much of the countryside, many of the walks around Waterside, and most important of all the Saturday night dances in the old wooden recreation hut at the other end of Clover Park. Many a Saturday afternoon was spent preparing for these, whitening our sandals and leaving them to dry on the boilers outside. These dances were presided over by James Innes sitting at a table by the door collecting entrance money and selling juice and crisps. Mr Innes was also the church officer. They were exciting and exuberant affairs with both modern and old time dancing. The eightsome reels were particularly wild and you were lucky, as a female, if you could keep your feet on the ground! The idea that they were alcohol free (many males arriving after the store bar closed) with the males seated down one side and the females down the other would seem strange to young people now.

It was at this point in our tour that I became particularly aware how individual memory can be either vague or selective and may need other people's memories as a trigger. I remember the Clover Park Cottage but not the house beyond and have forgotten who might have lived in either. I am told that the Dinwoodie family stayed in the former and Mr and Mrs Robert Forrester lived in the latter. Mr Forrester was senior in the accounting department of the Waterside National Coal Board (NCB) offices.

I do remember a great deal about the church such as Grandpa climbing the stairs into the pulpit at the beginning of services having been preceded by Mr Innes carrying the bible; the people who worshiped there (even if I need reminding of their names); confirmation classes and my confirmation; prize givings; Easter Sunday with new hats and outfits; bible class meetings; communion service; eating pan drops during the sermon and choking when Grandpa thumped the pulpit to emphasise a point, and the baptism of Edward, the younger of my two younger brothers. The last time I was inside was on Sunday 5th July 1970 to attend a memorial service for Grandpa conducted by the Rev. John Morton the minister from The Kirk of the Covenant in Dalmellington. At the end of the service Margaret Long gave me the flowers from the communion table to take home.

Most Sunday afternoons my mother, Laura, Robert and I would walk somewhere such as along the top line and over the fields to Patna and back by the main road; up and over the Green Hill, across to Keirs Farm; along the Dalmellington Road, or follow one of the routes to the Waterside Glen.

On summer Sundays when there was no evening service Grandpa often took me on a mystery bus tour and I saw a fair bit of Scotland this way. Remember this was when *bona fide* travelling on Sundays was popular! I was sorry not to be able to view the once very familiar stained glass windows above the pulpit and the rest of

St. Xavier's School in 1943. Perhaps the reader will be able to identify many of those in this photograph still living in the Doon Valley.
Back row: Jim McMahon, Maurice Mulholland, Michael Maguire, James Whalen, Margaret Maguire, Edward Higgins, James Hutchison, Gerald Mooney.
Middle row: Cathy Higgins, Rose Holland, Cathy Wallace, Matilda Whalen, Elizabeth Leitch, M Malone, Cathy Holland, Margaret Prendergast, Tessa O'Hagan and Ruby Bigham.
Front row: John Gilmour, John Rooney, Bertie McMahon, Jim Douglas and Tommy Gormanly.

the former church from inside but delighted to see that this place with so many memories was not derelict and looked well cared for.

Going back along Clover Park we walked down past the school gates and along to the right towards the Store – a once familiar journey. When we arrived in Waterside Laura went to school here, Robert to Patna and I went to Dalmellington. I have many memories of the grocery and drapery departments: friendly kindly people; butter and cheese in blocks on marble slabs; loose biscuits bought by the pound; wooden floors; old fashioned wooden counters; wooden and glass drawers and cupboards with all kinds of treasures in them; wool in hanks; ribbon in rolls; embroidery threads; needles; threads; shoes; underwear, and many other interesting and essential items. Sometimes I was sent down to ask the owner Mr John

MacDonald or his son Matt, as well as sometimes to the NCB offices, to cash Grandpa's very individual cheques written on whatever paper came to hand. Today's banks would love him! Perhaps next time this building and the station house next door will have been transformed. I understand the Ayrshire Railway Preservation Group has plans to restore the station but what about the Store? The stationmaster, James Johnstone, always kept the station and its gardens neat and tidy. Until we moved to Patna we were more likely to use the train to travel into Ayr usually on Saturdays. Janette was also responsible for introducing me to Ayr Skating Rink on Saturday mornings. I particularly remember the mischief in the corridorless train and the throwing of light bulbs over the viaduct on the return journey – I was too small to reach the sockets! On Saturday afternoons my mother would take us into Ayr, sometimes by train, to

the pictures so that Grandpa had peace to write his sermon.

The rows beside the store had gone by the time we arrived, all that was left were foundations and clothes poles but the New Cottages on the other side of the road were still there with one or two still occupied. I once met the visiting American relatives of someone who lived there in an old play park with swings somewhere here. The stables beside the New Cottages are still there and brought back memories of a horse that was stabled there. It and its master were a familiar sight delivering coal in the village. Their names were Jimmy and Wullie but I cannot remember which was which. Jeanie and Jimmy Robertson had the often-visited post office in the front room of one of the cottages in the now remaining row, the Monkey Row, on the main road. I particularly remember Mr Robertson who was a ballroom dancing

The tranquil River Doon at Waterside with a nice reflection.

enthusiast and, for a while, ran classes in the church hall.

Returning back up the hill and over the railway bridge towards Barley Park I was again impressed with the tidiness of the area, the well kept look of the houses and gardens as well as the provision of playground equipment. I do not remember the grass being so well kept, although I am sure it had been in its time. There were still a few people living in Barley Park during our time in Clover Park. Two in particular were the policeman and his family at our end and Mrs Reid further down. I used to go down to visit Mrs Reid once a week until she moved to Patna. She liked to bake and provided us with a variety of scones and other goodies every week. Visiting her house was a pleasurable experience, not only for the homemade lemonade, but just to sit and soak in the atmosphere. She had exquisite velvet covered antique chairs and other furniture as well as long luxurious seeming velvet curtains in front of the inset beds. I never visited her new house in Patna, but I hope she kept all her furniture.

In due course we moved to about halfway down Barley Park to a larger cottage with an inside lavatory and drinking water. This cottage was almost opposite the side gate to the school and very convenient for Laura. It was while we lived here that I got my first bike, a red Raleigh Boulevard Tourist, and with

it the freedom to explore further afield in the directions of Dalmellington, Loch Doon, Patna and other places. I was only ever at home if someone could catch me first! We also acquired our dog, Patch, one of the puppies of May Brown's dog. Mr and Mrs Colquhoun and their family, Margaret, Roy and Ian, were still living in Glenview at this time and Mr and Mrs Moore were the caretakers in the Miners' Institute. Two of the photos I still have are of Grandpa with the Colquhoun family when Ian was baptised. It was his first baptism in Waterside. Roy was in the class above me at Dalmellington and I have often wondered what he did when he left school. I still have contact with John Moore and still possess some of the books bought from the sale when the institute was closing.

After we left Barley Park the institute was used as the church hall and I remember many occasions there;

concerts, parties, socials, Burns suppers, church fetes, accompanying my mother from Patna to guild meetings, dancing lessons and the occasional Sunday School visit presided over by Tom Hose the Sunday School Superintendent. Sunday school picnics to the seaside were unforgettable experiences with excited chattering children; streamers flying from buses; community singing on the buses; pies and buns in brown paper bags; tea made in vast urns; the use of a church hall if it was raining; races of all kinds for all age groups; shopping for souvenirs and presents, and the company of the Dunaskin Brass band augmented by the Dalmellington Brass band. Outside the institute there was always the annual remembrance service. The restored institute seems an attractive and spacious private house from the outside and once again I would have loved to look inside. I was curious to see through the windows that what had been a large

The ruins of what was known as the Boatman's house on the west bank of the River Doon at Waterside.

By the time we walked back to the car park it was already after 4pm so a visit to the visitor centre had to wait until another day, but there was time to have a welcome cup of coffee and a slice of delicious cheese cake served by friendly staff in the Chimneys Restaurant as well as to purchase a book or two in the shop. No trip to the area, however, would be complete without a visit to my friend Ann O'Neil (ms Kennedy) in Dalmellington, so that was where we headed next. Again the left side of the road on the way to Dalmellington, particularly around the Chapel Row, seems silent and devoid of human life. It was always a hub of activity with men's voices and the noise of many pugs and bogies. The air would be filled with the unmistakable smell of slag being dumped at the foot of the glen and coal being delivered to the coal yard. On a previous occasion we stopped, had a walk around and visited the restored cottage. The RC school was still here when we lived in the village, as was the convent house where the priest and sisters lived. The cottage is like the ones we lived in, but there are differences. The main room of the cottage is similar to both, but the Clover Park cottages had a lobby leading off the main room with a bedroom on the left and a large press for food on the right. The kitchen and lavatory are in a similar position, but the boiler was outside the back window of the main room, not inside. In the Barley Park

billiard room and then the main church hall now has large doors at the stage end and houses a caravan. The owners of the former church should, perhaps, think about charging entrance to the nosey people like me! The garden is very tidy and attractive but what access do the public have to the well cared for War Memorial now included in this garden?

Eventually we received the news, first from Annie the post (Annie McClymont), and then in the letter she handed Grandpa that we had been allocated the tenancy of a new SHA house in Patna. Annie was a familiar person during these two years and there were many stories associated with her. The day came when our belongings were loaded onto the back of a lorry and we flitted to 2 Keirs Crescent Patna aided by many kind and willing ex-Waterside residents. But this was not the end of our association with Waterside. Grandpa was still the minister and often I walked the

road with him on Sunday mornings so that we were in church before the buses carrying the congregation from Patna arrived. We had many long discussions about the meaning of life and other topics during these walks.

An old man called Harry Boswell lived in Barley Park Cottage but although I saw him on many occasions I did not know him to talk to. The Green Hill Row was still there but I cannot remember anyone living there. When we moved to Patna, like other people, many of our first garden plants came from the old gardens and these ones were a rich source. It would be interesting to still be able to walk along the paths which lay behind and between where Clover Park, Barley Park, Green Hill Rows and their coal sheds were, but these areas are full of a variety of young trees and bushes. Much has changed, but Waterside is still a very beautiful place.

Burnton Washer circa 1950 looking towards Chalmerston. This is where the coal was screened before being transported to various destinations by train.

cottage, which was the other way round, there was only one bedroom that was the size of both Chapel Row front parlour and bedroom put together. It had an extra room that led off the living room and which may have been the original scullery. This room had a door on the right which led to a glass covered passage. The scullery door was directly opposite this room with the lavatory at the end of the passage, on the left, beside the back door. It had no brick boiler, as grid electricity had arrived by that time, so my mother acquired an electric one. Both the scullery and the corridor appeared to have been tagged onto the back of the cottage at a later date.

It is only in retrospect that I realise how privileged I have been to have experienced the last days of Waterside as an industrial village. At the time it seemed so unlike anywhere else we had lived that other places and my past life took on an unrealistic quality. I think though we were soon accepted and we did settle down reasonably well. John and I will be back and on other occasions may be able not only to visit the visitor centre, but to walk along the top railway track as far as the incline to Lethanhill and maybe walk up it to where the village had been; continue along the railway track and see if it is still possible to walk to Patna across the fields; climb the Green Hill (I am not sure if I still

have the stamina as I remember it as being a never ending climb); visit the Ardoon woods in the spring; explore more of the glen; visit Keir's castle and monitor restoration progress.

It has been an interesting experience not only to retrace personal memories but also to realise that individual memory is only one part of the story. It may need a variety of triggers to draw a fuller picture. I have left some things out deliberately but curiously it is mostly the best about the place and the people that I remember. I just hope their memories of me and mine are mostly as kindly and friendly as mine.

*A high sun slanting
its escape through canopies
of leaf and cloud
seeks out a skylight
to this glade of buttercups.
Bright sun-soaked petals
newly glazed reflect
A buttery beam
on smiling chins.*

*Like us, the flowers span
but the briefest blink of time:
no grand design, just
generations linked
haphazardly:
seeds on the wind
and dusty layers
of unnoteworthy lives.*

*But in the other's eye
for just the briefest moment
of belonging, we too reflect
a smile, exquisitely.*

De Luca, Christine (1995): *Voes and Sounds* Shetland Library Lerwick p29

CHAPTER 11

PATNA AND THE 'HILL

Two miles north of Waterside is the village of Patna sitting quietly on both sides of the scenic River Doon. Pont's map of 1600 marked 'Preestoun' in the Doon Valley some 15 km south east of Ayr. There was also a Milton nearby and a road existed up the valley by the time the Roy map was made in the middle of the 18th century. Polnessan, nearby was the site of the ford across the river. The name Patna was of recent origin and was only introduced in the early 19th century. Wilson avers that the name is derived from *Pait 'n Ath*, the water of the eminence, for the old village is built upon a steep hillside west of the river although it has expanded considerably on the east bank in recent years. Moore suggests that the village was founded in the early 19th century and owes its name to the great city on the Ganges through links with a local landowner and industrialist, William Fullarton, whose family had close associations with India.

Like its near neighbours, Patna relied heavily on coal mining and remained a very small village until the inhabitants of Lethanhill and Waterside were rehoused there in the mid 1950s. The population today is around 3,000.

It is generally accepted that 1802 is the founding date of the village when prosperous local businessman, Mr William Fullarton of Skeldon, provided employment to many local people in his coal and limestone pits in the area. He was described as a very dark, handsome and powerful man and was known by locals as "Black Willie," because of his dark features. He was said to have been very fond of jewellery and being a rich man, he wore a number of rings on his fingers. He had a fiery temper and anyone who worked for him had a fear of being called up to the green table in his offices in Patna's Main Street.

However, what cannot be denied is that he was a great benefactor to the district and his decision to begin mining along the extensive outcrops of coal along what is still known as the "Bank" on the edge of the Doon towards the Mill was good news for local men seeking employment. He appointed a manager who took up residence in what became known locally as Patna House. This house with offices attached was located in Collier Row later known as the High Row; which had disappeared before 1920.

One particularly useful and popular service provided for villagers by Fullarton was the construction of a wooden pipeline which ran from Craignessie Well located near to Patna cemetery into the village. He later built a schoolhouse for the village.

William Fullarton was born in India in 1774, his father was Major-General John Fullarton of the East India Company who had two sons, William and Robert. The latter died at the age of five. It was in 1801 that Fullarton purchased Skeldon estate, which extended at that time as far

O' a' ye Bards on bonie Doon!
An wha on Ayr your chanters tune!
Come, join the melancholious croon
O' Robin's reed!

Poor Mailies Elegy
Robert Burns

Prize winners at Lethanhill Flying Club early 1960s. The folk on the 'Hill had a variety of social and recreational organisations, pigeons being very popular.
Back row (l to r): Hugh Ferguson, James Mulholland, Johnny Gillespie, Harry Graham, Andrew Steele
Front row: John Givens, Mrs Steele, John Boyle, Billy Pettigrew, May Mulholland

westwards as Carskeoch, where he had limekilns, the ruins of which can still be seen. He sold it again to the Hon. Mrs Leslie Cumming in 1828, and in the same year he was elected Provost of Ayr. He married Susan, daughter of the celebrated Dr Whiteside of Ayr, and they had a family of six sons and seven daughters. In 1805 he was responsible for the construction of Patna Bridge (The Auld Brig). The architect was Mr Gilbert McAdam, a relative of the inventive engineer who gave his name to the world-famous tar-surfacing for roads. The bridge's structure is lasting testimony to the craftsmen of these early days. In January 1835 Fullarton died aged 60 and was buried in the cemetery of Ayr Auld Kirk. He is remembered in Ayr and Patna with streets named in his honour.

The Walker Fountain is located in Patna's Main Street. The fountain was gifted to the people of Patna by Major A Barclay Walker of Liverpool, a partner in the firm of Peter Walker and Son, brewers, Worthington and the formal opening ceremony was held on 18 August, 1872. The fountain is inscribed:

"Presented by A Barclay Walker, Esquire, to the inhabitants of Patna." The design was by Henry H Vale, architect, Liverpool. Subsequently the top of the fountain was removed because of recurring vandalism. The day of the inauguration of the fountain was a great occasion for the villagers with all the principal streets decorated with banners, bunting and floral tributes. The weather was excellent and a great crowd gathered as Major and Mrs Walker were met by a brass band as they arrived with friends from Ayr in four carriages. The Rev Thomas McFadzean gave a lengthy address in the name of the people of Patna and he referred to the old fountain which had been given to the village by William Fullarton of Skeldon seventy years before. The fountain was formally opened by Miss Walker, daughter of the Major and she was presented with a silver cup as a token of esteem on behalf of the villagers of Patna. The

event was described in the Ayr Advertiser as, "a bright and memorable day in the history of Patna." Major Walker also owned Camlarg Estate, Dalmellington.

In the early years of Patna there was no bridge spanning the river and access to the east side of the river where the early village began was by boat until the Auld Bridge was built in 1805. The first house in the village was built about 1803 a year later than Patna House which was occupied by Mr Gilbert McAdam who designed Patna Old Bridge.

By 1837 the first real church building came on the scene with the establishment of the United Free Church. Interestingly, the present building most folk will know as the Wheatsheaf Hotel came into being in the much more austere role of Manse before the building of the hotel. Houses then gradually began to appear on the

scene on the west bank of the river, all of them being single-storied buildings; for it was not until the turn of the century that the upper stories began to make an appearance.

In 1900 the sinking of the nearby Houldsworth colliery was completed on behalf of the Dalmellington Iron Company at a cost of a quarter of a million sterling, and this brought an immediate and very marked change to the district. Here was employment in abundance for the men and for their sons to follow in their footsteps. But of course mining was demanding, hard and exacting work. This colliery was noted for its top grade steam-coal. Wages in the coal industry were very poor, but the benefit for the miners was continuity of employment.

Another major change came about in 1927 when Ayr County Council erected the first council houses at Jellieston to be followed by others in Patna's Lower Main Street. In the early days of Patna, like so many other villages in Ayrshire of that era, water had to be drawn from wells and carried into the home in pails. Times were indeed changing and by 1937 the nearby hamlet of Kerse was demolished and its small population rehoused in new buildings at Polnessan, Main Street, Patna and Dalrymple.

The war years between 1939-1945 meant that progress virtually ground to a halt because every inch of timber and ounce of metal was required for the war effort. The domestic requirements of local folk were not regarded as important in these austere times. After the war there was an even greater demand for housing and this resulted in prefabricated buildings being quickly erected in most small villages in Ayrshire. These 'prefabs' as they were known were small but very comfortable and residents regarded them with great affection, most of them having lasted well beyond their expected lifetime.

In the Autumn of 1947, the first families were removed from Lethanhill and Burnfoothill, (known conveniently simply as the Hill), to Doonbank Terrace, Patna and "Operation Flitting" had began in earnest as the folk of the hill villages moved down into the valley, some leaving with great reluctance. After all, this close-knit community sitting high above the River Doon was all they had ever known as home. Many had been born and raised here. Their fathers, grandfathers and great grandfathers lived there. These lasting bonds with family and friends of yesteryear made many families reluctant to move, although the living conditions in their homes on the hill were basic. Before long, however, Lethanhill was depopulated and later reduced to rubble. Nearby Waterside had also became two rather lonely and dejected rows of houses. Although Lethanhill, which began its life in 1851, was being gradually depopulated and finally abandoned, this process was only completed in 1954.

Eve Mulholland and Frank Osborne in 1963. They are on the A713 Ayr – Dalmellington Road between Patna and Polnessan, a favourite place for drifting snow to block the road. The two youngsters lived in Polnessan.

Benwhat's David 'Dunty' Dunsmuir in his boxing days. He joined City of Glasgow Police and was a great Burns enthusiast. He died in the 1970s.

Interestingly, the hill senior secondary school remained operational until 1959 when the pupils were then transferred to Dalmellington High School. The last headmaster was Mr Donohoe who lived in the house at Lethanhill, the only dwelling which remains to this day. Perhaps saddest of all acts was the laying

down of a substantial sitka spruce plantation on the site of the hill village covering the ruins which were home to generations of hardy folk. Visitors today entering the plantation will be moved to find wreaths and flowers laid on the ground, in trees or on the foundations of houses by loved ones who still remember those of yesteryear who were part of that special breed of men who lived on the plateau high above the valley of Doon.

The opening of what became known as The New Bridge across the Doon took place on 25 March, 1960. It was the first to be built in the County entirely from Ayr County Council funds. This bridge enabled improved access into Patna from the A713 and there was a boom in building Council houses in the 1960s and 1970s which left the west bank of Patna largely as it is today. The building of private houses on the east side of the A713 occurred in the 1980s and 1990s

with these private developments allowing local folk to purchase their own homes and also enabling new families to move into Patna.

Patna today is really a composite community made up of folk from six distinct groups – Patna, Kerse, Lethanhill/Burnfoothill, Waterside, newcomers from the Lanarkshire coalfields and latterly folk making a positive choice to move to Patna to live in the new private houses built on the east side of the A713. There is an excellent nine hole golf course located to the east of the River Doon and a small number of public houses and social clubs in the village. A former garment factory closed in 2000 and re-opened in 2002 manufacturing products for the health-care industry. Like its near neighbours, Patna would benefit greatly from more local employment. And in acknowledgement of its somewhat

A view of Lethanhill from the home of Mr George Donohoe, headmaster of the village school. The boy dressed to celebrate the Coronation in 1953 is Brian Donohoe, the headmaster's son and now Member of Parliament for Cunninghame South. The long row coming from the left of the photo is Polnessan Road, Burnfoothill. The building in the centre is the the 'New School' which was a secondary school until its closure in 1959. The building on the right was originally the village hall and later it became the dining hall of the school.

A lone walker tramps along the path at Step Row, Lethanhill. The Old School immediately on left of path and the ruin of the Village hall immediately to the left of the old school.

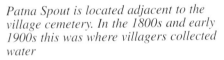

Patna Spout is located adjacent to the village cemetery. In the 1800s and early 1900s this was where villagers collected water

tenuous links with Patna, India, Robert Burns has fitting words to end this brief overview of Patna, Ayrshire.

O' could I give thee India's wealth,
As I this trifle send!
Because the Joy in both would be
To share them with a friend!

To John McMurdo Esq of Drumlanrig
Robert Burns

CHAPTER 12
CHILDHOOD MEMORIES OF LETHANHILL – A GHOST VILLAGE

By Ann MacLean (Donohoe)

Amidst thy desert walks the lapwing flies,
And tires their echoes with unvaried cries.
Sunk are thy bowers, in shapeless ruin all,
And the long grass o'ertops the mouldering wall.

The Deserted Village
Oliver Goldsmith

Lethanhill Church and School as many former villagers and pupils will remember it. The village was finally abandoned in 1954, but interestingly the school remained open until 1959.

Ann Donohoe arrived in Lethanhill, age 7 when the village was in terminal decline. She left age 15 what was by then a deserted village, the whole population having been re-housed in the Doon Valley, mainly in Patna. Ann married Donald MacLean in Irvine in 1966 and they have two sons, Niall and Colin. They have lived very happily in Kilmaurs for many years. She worked as a secretary in Ayrshire Metal Products Irvine for some 10 years and thereafter became a full-time housewife and mother. She is very involved in voluntary work and is an elder and assistant convener of the Guild in Laigh West High Kirk, Kilmarnock. Keen on flower arranging, she thoroughly enjoys this hobby and has occasionally been persuaded to create floral arrangements for weddings. She loves music, and has been singing in choirs for most of her life. She is now thoroughly enjoying retirement with her husband, Donald. Her second youngest brother is Brian Donohoe MP for Cunninghame South whose formative years were also spent at Lethanhill. All the Donohoe family are very proud of their association with Lethanhill. They still enjoy taking a journey down memory lane to visit their former home, now a private dwelling, and the remains of the ghost village on the high moors above the River Doon.

George and Catherine Donohoe moved to Lethanhill from Kilmaurs in October 1951 with their three children. I was the eldest aged seven and my brothers George and Brian were five and three respectively. Dad, who was the new Headmaster of the Junior Secondary School had travelled from Kilmaurs, (a journey involving three different buses) for some considerable time before the schoolhouse at Lethanhill was ready for the family to live in.

Shortly before leaving Kilmaurs, Dad learned to drive and became the proud owner of a second hand Hillman saloon. Although the houses at Lethanhill had electricity installed in 1926, our newly decorated schoolhouse was without electric power. Lighting was by calor gas, and the kitchen was kept cosy by a Rayburn stove, from which Mum produced mouth-watering meals and superb baking.

Washing was done by hand with the help of an Acme wringer. To iron clothes, she used a heavy calor gas iron, with gas jets round the inside of the base, always having to be especially careful when ironing garments with fringing or frills, in case the gas jets singed them. There was of course no television set, but we enjoyed listening to the battery powered radio.

Our water supply came from a hillside storage tank to which lime was added from time to time to purify it. After such

A nostalgic view of Lethanhill School looking from the Store Row to the ruin of the Village Store and immediately behind it is the old school to the left and on the right is the village hall which was used latterly as a dining room and PE hall for the school. The building on the far right is the New School which was a Junior Secondary School which closed its doors for the last time in December 1959.

A fancy dress parade was held in Lethanhill Hall just at end of the Second World War
When the children of the village donned fancy dress to celebrate and win prizes. This photos is taken outside the 'Hill church.
(l to r): Helen Knox (McLelland), Margaret Knox, Billy Johnstone (Winston Churchhill) and Jean Knox (McDickens). Billy Johnstone won the prize.

treatment the water looked like fizzy lemonade. On fortunately rare occasions, small frogs would emerge from the taps.

During the summer, if there had been a dry spell of weather we could be completely without water. This normally happened during the school holiday, when thankfully we were able to use the school's storage supply, sometimes going into the cookery room to have a good wash in the large deep sinks.

On my first day at Lethanhill School the other pupils were very friendly and welcoming. The teacher for my class, which was a composite class of primary three and four was Miss Parker. At playtime the girls formed a large circle singing such songs as 'The big ship sails through the Illy Ally-O', 'Water water wallflower', 'I sent a letter to my love' and 'In and out those dusty bluebells'. When the weather was fine we would

draw beds on the playground and play with peevers or use skipping ropes, one of the many songs we used to sing was 'Oh there she goes, Oh there she goes, Peery heels and pointed toes, look at her feet, she thinks she's neat, black stockings and dirty feet'.

At other times we would bring a couple of tennis or small rubber balls and bounce them off the wall singing 'Plainy, clappy, rolly, backy etc'. The boys played with marbles, peashooters, and conkers, but were always happiest kicking a ball about. We often played rounders, tig, or hide and seek.

The moor was an exciting extension of the playground. At weekends and holidays there was always plenty to do to fill our time. We played with metal fenders turned up at the front, using them like sledges to slide down the grassy slopes. Playing in the burn was great fun. Having races

using empty tin cans, looking for frog spawn, or trying to build a dam.

In the spring we used to help the shepherd set the moors on fire, the lovely smell of burning grass filling the air.

Lethanhill School circa 1952
Back row (l to r): Miss Parker (teacher), Galt, David Ferguson, rest unknown.
Second row: Hugh Kennedy, ?, Thomson, Wilma Cran, Janette Gillespie, Ann Donohoe (McLean), Marion Bryden and George Murray.
Front row: Madge Galloway, McDonald, Graham, Mary Johnstone (Robson), Jean Knox (Cole),

Lethanhill School staff circa 1951
Back row: Matt McLellan and Jimmy Paterson
Front: William Fawcett, janitor, Sadie McIndoe formerly of Smithston Farm who was the domestic science teacher, George Donohoe (headmaster). At that time in addition to those in the photo there was Miss Faulder (infant mistress) and other teachers.

There was always a breeze blowing on the Hill, ideal for flying kites. Making a kite was a serious business, needing brown paper, canes, and paste with old newspaper and string for the tail. Some flew better than others, soaring to great heights before diving to the ground, startling any sheep that may have been grazing nearby.

Some distance behind the school was a disused quarry where there were still some tracks with bogies lying around. In the quarry, which was at least 1,000 feet above sea level, we found fossils of shells, showing us that the sea had at one time covered the area. We must have walked for miles, going by foot to visit friends down in Patna, or to the sweetie shop on Saturdays to spend some of our pocket money. I can remember after a winter shopping trip to Ayr with my Mum, getting off the bus at the foot of the hill at Downieston Farm. I was about ten at the time, it was very dark, and I must confess that I was just a little scared walking up the road, and hearing strange sounds, my imagination running riot.

A date in history which I will always remember, was the Coronation of Queen Elizabeth. To commemorate the great event on June 2, 1953 the pupils of my age were presented with a long flat metal box which had a picture of the Queen on the lid. The box was filled with Cadburys chocolates and was to be used as a pencil case afterwards. Some of the younger children were presented with Coronation mugs and the older girls were given brooches in the shape of a crown with red, white and blue stones. There was a special Coronation Gala day in Patna with Queen Lily Gilmour and attendants. The school children were asked to come in fancy dress. Mum was kept busy before the big day making our outfits.

The outside of the schoolhouse was decorated red white and blue as was the car. We received a prize of £1, which was quite something at that time. One of my brothers still has the note, which is twice the size of today's notes. In August of

Donohoe family at Lethanhill Schoolhouse circa 1958.
(l to r): Brian Donohoe, 9, Catherine Donohoe, John Donohoe, 4, George Donohoe, headmaster of Lethanhill School, Ann Donohoe, 14 and George Donohoe, 12.

The headmasters house at Lethanhill with Ann, Brian in the car and George Donohoe in 1953 preparing for the Coronation celebrations on 2 June. This house remains the only inhabited dwelling at Lethanhill today.

that year my youngest brother John was born at Lethanhill. I can remember proudly pushing him in his pram past some derelict houses so that a friend who was still in the village could see him.

The process of re-housing all the people of Lethanhill and Burnfoothill took seven years. The first families were allocated houses in Patna at the end of 1947 and by summer 1954 the last person had moved and the once busy rows were completely deserted and forlorn. It was really quite sad, especially for our family who were the only family to remain on the Hill.

When Dad had come to Lethanhill as Headmaster, the younger primary pupils were taught in the 'Old School' which was built in 1912 and had three classrooms. Older primary children along with secondary pupils were taught in the 'New School', which when opened in

1928 was one of the most modern and well equipped schools in the County of Ayrshire. However, within a year or two of him being appointed Headmaster most families had moved to Patna. The influx of primary age children was more than Patna school could cope with, so it was arranged that nine to eleven year old pupils would be taken by bus from Patna and taught in the 'Old School' at Lethanhill. They were regularly visited by Mr. Baird, Headmaster of Patna Primary who's often repeated mantra to his pupils was 'Speed, - Accuracy, - Neatness!'

This arrangement continued until larger schools were built at Patna. For this reason, around 120 secondary pupils were also being bussed back up the hill from Patna to the 'New School' building.

Although the miners rows at Lethanhill lay in ruins, the sound of young people's

voices and much laughter echoed round the deserted village during the school term, which was quite strange when you think of it now. At other times the bleating of sheep, the cry of peewits and skylarks in the summer skies were the only sounds to be heard.

I have a photograph of the Donohoe family taken early in 1958 at Lethanhill

which I treasure. This, as well as the one of the schoolhouse and the other of the two schools, was shown on Cliff Michelmore's Television programme, 'To-night'. Our parents had been asked to go to the BBC studios in Glasgow to be interviewed for the programme. This had come about because of an article in the national press. Dad had refused to sign the missive of let for the schoolhouse, as he wished to move to more satisfactory housing in Ayr. However, the 'powers that be' decided that he must 'stay put' in Lethanhill, albeit we were the only residents living on the high moorland with a deserted and ruined village as our nearby neighbour. The new secondary school at Patna wasn't going to be completed for another year or two, and until then the Education committee were not prepared to relieve him of his obligation to live in the schoolhouse.

In the summer of 1959 we moved to Irvine. Dad had been appointed Headmaster of Loudon Montgomery Primary school, a post he filled until his retirement. We lived in the Lethanhill Schoolhouse for eight years. As a youngster that seemed like a lifetime. However, we have many happy memories of the 'Hill' and of friends we made during our stay. We have all taken our families back to see where we grew up and in brother John's case, where he was born. It is heart-warming to think back to those happy childhood days.

But now the sounds of population fail,
No cheerful murmurs fluctuate in the gale,
No busy steps the grass-worn footway tread,
For all the bloomy flush of life is fled.

The Deserted Village
Oliver Goldsmith

Brian Donohoe stayed in Lethanhill for a relatively short time, but has very fond memories of this Hill village. He lived in the Schoolhouse with his mother and father, sister Ann and brother George. His younger brother, John, was born on the 'Hill on the 8th August 1953. Brian was about 2-3 years old when the family moved to Lethanhill and he remembers going to Patna Primary in 1953 and on to Waterside Primary where his teacher in Primary 5 was Mrs Scott who stayed in Waterside, the wife of Louis Scott, well known in the Doon Valley. His teacher in Primary 6 was Miss Lennox. The Head Teacher was Mr Taylor who went on to become the Headmaster of Lethanhill for a very short period when Brian's father George and the family left in 1958/59. Brian worked as an Apprentice fitter/turner in Ailsa Shipbuilding Troon on a wage of £3-19s-1d. He was one of the two apprentices to be sent for a year to the Government Training Centre in Irvine. He then served his apprenticeship firstly in the fitting side going into the Machine Shop and then into the Drawing Office until being made redundant in 1977. He recalls that this was probably the best thing that ever happened to him and one of the reasons he became so interested in politics. He became a Member of Parliament in 1992 for Cunninghame South and has served on the Transport Select Committee since 25th January 1993. He was re-elected to the new seat of Central Ayrshire from 5th May 2005. Like the rest of his family, Brian has many fond memories of living at the 'Hill and indeed was the principal speaker at the final Lethanhill Reunion.

Ann McLean now lives in Kilmaurs. She is the sister of Brian Donohoe MP. She recalls her happy childhood days at Lethanhill where he father George was headmaster of the village school.

Travelling from Dalmellington to Ayr on the A713 we quickly pass through Hollybush. The journey along the tree-lined main road obscures some very fine and imposing large mansion houses. Indeed the small village is really a crossroads hamlet. Hollybush House, originally Over Skeldon, is of 1853 vintage, by Robert Paton. This Elizabethan house is now used as a rehabilitation and respite home for ex servicemen, having previously been a hotel for several years. Nearby is Skeldon House which dates from circa 1780. This is a typically elegant house of the period, with advanced and pedimented centre bays to both front and rear, with fine neo-Georgian additions of 1908 by James Millar. This grand house is situated in extensive woodland, which drops steeply down to the River Ayr. Just off the road to Dalrymple is Balgreen which is a fine example of an early model farm, a square red stone steading by Robert Ingram. This farm had a fine reputation for breeding Clydesdale horses, but nowadays the interest is purely retained as a hobby. The Hollybush Inn is a popular restaurant on the A713 slightly to the north of the main village and caters for a range of social functions.

Hollybush was even able to boast its own railway station when the ill-fated Ayrshire and Galloway Railway Company began construction of a line to Dalmellington. Financial problems besieged the company, but by 1856 their successors in the form of the Glasgow and South Western Railway Company finally completed and opened the branch

"And were thou this" – she solemn said,
And bound the holly round my head:
The polish'd leaves and berries red
Did rustling play;
And, like a passing thought, she fled
In light away.

The Vision
Robert Burns

The G & SW branch line from Ayr to Dalmellington at Holehouse Junction. The Rankinston line is on the right. This was simply an exchange platform with no external access.

The Ayr - Dalmellington Branch line at Holehouse Junction near Hollybush is closed due to heavy snow fall on 1st January 1940. The men are working to remove the snow and reopen the line.

line to Dalmellington. The station in Hollybush opened to passenger traffic on 7th August that year. The rail passenger service was withdrawn on 6th April 1964 to all stations on the branch line. Interestingly, although the line is no longer used for passenger traffic, it is an exceptionally busy mineral line with two or more trains per day operating to Minnivey Loading Point where coal is loaded on to around 30 wagons per train. Indeed during 2002 major structural work lasting for six months was carried out on the Burnton Viaduct at Dalrymple thereby ensuring that trains can continue to slowly snake through the Valley of Doon for many years to come.

The once world famous Skeldon Mills was the only employer of note in Hollybush and it closed its doors to blanket making in the 1950s. Skeldon lies on the north bank of the River Doon, 3km east of Dalrymple and 10 km south

east of Ayr. The area was already thickly settled when mapped by Timothy Pont around 1600 and there was a castle recorded in Hollybush, no longer extant. Here the River Doon winds its way past Hollybush House to Skeldon, famous for

its blankets which were sent round the world bearing the label 'Made By Ye Banks And Braes o' Bonnie Doon.' The mills employed mainly women but had a reputation for producing world-acclaimed blankets and the name Skeldon became

Cairntable was a small hamlet, no longer extant, between Polnessan and Drongan. Most of the men worked in the local coal mines such as nearby Littlemill. This is an early 1900s photo and the villagers were probably asked to assemble for the benefit of the photographer. The railway bridge can be seen in the background. This ran from Holehouse Junction to Mauchline.

Kerse Store with three staff at the front. This was one of the stores operated by the Dalmellington Iron Company. Today at Kerse there is only two private houses, both built in recent years.

an industry standard for quality. There are now several small factory outlets operating from Skeldon Mills and a caravan site located by the picturesque River Doon, recently closed.

Hollybush village saw an increase in private house building in the 1970s and 1980s, but the small village school closed before 1980 as did the village post office. Villagers now travel to Dalrymple or Ayr for day to day shopping and the village is really a dormitory hamlet, considered by residents as a really good place to live.

Wit and Grace and love and beauty
In ae constellation shine!
To adore thee is my duty,
Goddess o this soul o mine.

Bonny Wee Thing
Robert Burns

Benston Smiddy stands on the A713 north of Hollybush. A blacksmith has operated from here for many years.

Tongue Row about 1920s. This small row of houses was located on the road between Polnessan and Littlemill. Less than half a mile below was Cairntable. Tongue Row was abandoned about 1930 and the inhabitants rehoused at Polnessan and Dalrymple.

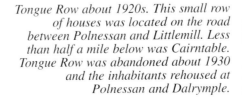

CHAPTER 14
DALRYMPLE

Among the bonie winding banks,
Where Doon rins, wimplin, clear:
Where Bruce ance ruled the martial
ranks,
An shook his Carrick spear.

Halloween
Robert Burns

Dalrymple village lies on the north bank of the River Doon, 8 km south of Ayr. The area was already densely settled when mapped by Pont around 1600. However, at that time there was no bridge to the imposing and emparked 14th century castle of Cassillis, 2 km downstream on the south bank, and Dalrymple seems not to have attracted early travel writers.

The kirk at Dalrymple is located on the western edge of the village near to the River Doon. It is a fairly small, yet dignified building. It dates in its present form to around 1855, although local records suggest that a church stood on this site for centuries. King James IV (reigned 1488 - 1513), gifted the church and its teinds to the Chapel Royal of Stirling. The present building is Gothic in style and has two prominent stained glass windows by Stephen Adam and Son. In 1964 a new vestry and session house were added to the kirk, designed by Robert Calderwood who was born at the famous Purclewan Mill in the parish. The cost of this extension was the gift of Miss M Reid, organist from 1950 - 1957. The current minister is Reverend James Crighton and Henry Murdoch is session clerk.

The name Dalrymple is generally believed to derive from the Gaelic *Dail a' Chruim Puill* which is translated as "flat field of the crooked pool or river," which is indeed a fairly accurate description of the area around this level village which is surrounded by low undulating hills. In the Statistical Account of 1791, the Rev Ebenezer Walker makes an interesting if somewhat ambiguous claim for the village. He states that the name means "the valley of the slaughter of the king," and avers that it is supposed that Coilus (Old King Cole) was killed here. Whilst this is an interesting theory it is probably quite spurious and the earlier Gaelic translation is likely to have a more solid foundation.

Interestingly, Charles S Dougal's book, The Burns Country (1904) tells of early historians describing a great battle at the "Water of Dun" in Carrick, in which Maximus and the Romans defeated Eugenius, King of Scots. "Most of the Scottish leaders were slain, and were buried on the field. Stone coffins and cairns, and the remnants of British forts, found on the banks of Doon near the village of Dalrymple, suggest a site for this almost forgotten battle." The likelihood is that myth and legend have come together to create a fascinating story and it would take some convincing archaeological finds to provide compelling evidence to give credibility to the claim. Conversely, the rich history of south west Scotland tells of Bruce and Wallace being regularly in the area, so it may not be too far fetched to suggest that this was indeed an area which witnessed important battles, now long forgotten.

The village of Dalrymple is, however, of fairly recent lineage. Prior to 1800 there was virtually no village of any substance

Skeldon House is located on the southern edge of Dalrymple near the site of what was known as Nether Skeldon Castle. This 18th century country seat is a three storey plus attic classical mansion of five bays. The house was probably built by Major General John Fullarton who is said to have made many improvements to the estate. The current owner since 1986 is Stanley E Brodie, QC. The formal gardens adjacent to the River Doon are simply stunning.

on this site other than a few cottages around the church. The village was developed by the local laird who laid out the two main thoroughfares – Main Street and Garden Street – and erected the cottages which today are still a very attractive feature of the village. The village seems to have grown very slowly until after the Second World War when the old mining communities within the parish such as Kerse, Tongue Row and Cairntable were gradually abandoned and the miners moved to new houses in Dalrymple. The population of the parish in 1755 was 439 rising by 1821 to 933 and today's figure is around 1600. At the time of the Statistical Account in 1791 the parish had 86 inhabited houses, forty of which were occupied by farmers. There were six weavers, three shoemakers, two smiths, one wright and one tailor. A farm labourer earned around tenpence to one and fivepence per day. Coal and peat sold at around 4d to 6d per load.

The Dalrymple Friendly Society was formed in 1807. The rules stated that there had to be at least 60 members who contributed a fixed sum into the funds at regular intervals. This money was used to support members who, through sickness or disablement, were unable to work and they received six shillings per week if they were so unfit that they were unable to leave the house. However, those who were not quite so incapacitated and were able to leave the home received four shillings per week. Medical opinion had to confirm the situation before any money was paid. Should a member die, the other members contributed one shilling each to defray funeral costs. Interestingly, the society chairman would act as chief mourner if a member died and had no relations.

In 1891 only 300 people lived in the village. Remarkably, by 1951 the population of Dalrymple had risen to

1,175. By 1971 this had risen further to about 1,525, with all the facilities so necessary for a thriving village including a first-class hotel and bowling green. However, by 1991 the population had fallen back to around 1,300. This may almost certainly have risen again with the building of private dwellinghouses in the village in the late 1990s.

Burns described the nearby hill of Dunree on the Carrick side of the River Doon in his poem Halloween as Cassillis Downans where the fairies play:

Amang the bonie winding banks,
Where Doon rins, wimplin' clear...

On many occasions over the years the Doon, being located close to the western flank of the village, has flooded causing considerable damage. On 14 January 1814 the river burst its banks with frightening ferocity and flooded homes to a level of three feet. Many of the villagers had to leave their homes and the local headmaster, Mr Campbell, took the displaced villagers into the schoolhouse where they remained until the flooding

The famous River Doon as it passes the policies of Skeldon House.

subsided and they were eventually able to return to their homes.

The Marquis of Ailsa owned about half of the land in the parish in the early part of the 19th century. It was he who was responsible for building the neat cottages in Main and Garden Streets. Prior to that the houses around the church would have been of very basic design and would have been thatched.

Skeldon House is an imposing mansion house located close to the village. It was built near to the site of Nether Skeldon Castle, sometime in the 18th century. This building is a fine three storey plus attic classical mansion of five bays, with an unusual entrance portico at first floor level. It is believed that the house was built by Major General John Fullarton, who made many improvements to the estate. One of the owners of Skeldon House was James Weir (linked to the famous Glasgow engineering firm, Weirs of Cathcart) who took over the mansion in 1926. He died in 1973, his wife Moira in 1980. Moira was an enterprising and very brave lady. J S McChesney in *The Story of Dalrymple*, suggests that Moira was the first lady to obtain a flying certificate and, along with a Spaniard named Juan de La Cierva, made numerous experiments with an Autogyro, which was the forerunner of the helicopter. Moira Weir used Barbieston Holm, now a plantation, as her airfield where she built a large hanger to store the aircraft. One of the earliest

helicopter flights in Britain is reputed to have taken place at Dalrymple on 7th June 1938, in a Weir W-5. Skeldon House is now owned by Mr Stanley Brodie QC who acquired the estate in 1985 adding Balgreen in 1987 and Yonderton in 1989. In 2005 he further enlarged the estate by adding Potterston Farm extending the estate to 870 acres. The grounds of this imposing mansion house are simply stunning with the River Doon forming a 'U' bend bordering the formal and beautifully maintained gardens adjacent to this famous salmon river. The writer had the privilege of being shown round the gardens by Mr Brodie in June, 2005. The gardens are open to the public at least once each year and this is widely advertised.

The Ayr – Dalmellington Railway was opened in May 1856 for goods and in August for passengers and a station was established at Hollybush some two miles to the south of the village. Dalrymple had its own station, but unfortunately it was located just over 1 mile from the village at Carcluie and opened on 1 November 1856. Consequently it was not at all convenient. It was set on what was then the Ayr and Maybole Railway, later part of the Glasgow and South Western Railway. The station was closed on 6 December 1954 but the removal of this service had little impact on the village which was well served by 'buses into Ayr.

Being a rural community, agriculture was traditionally a large employer of local labour and corn, roots, potatoes and cabbage were widely grown in the parish at the time of the statistical account of 1791. Most of the land was under grazing, mainly cattle, though the eastern moors had many sheep. However, with modern farming methods requiring fewer and fewer workers the trend today is that most farms are worked by the farmer and his family. Indeed it is common that farmers are often part-time on the land and working elsewhere to enable them to afford to carry on farming.

Like most other Doon Valley villages, coal was worked on a small scale. Kerse Pits (Nos 1 and 2) were operated by the Cairntable Gas and Coal Company with headquarters in Bothwell Street, Glasgow. In 1913 this was a busy operation with 134 men working below ground supported by 27 above. Various shafts were sunk, one in the late 1800s, one in 1910, another in 1913, but they were all closed by the end of the Great War.

Dalrymple is the village nearest to Mount Oliphant Farm where Robert Burns lived, worked and socialised from age 7 to 18 years. The Bard undoubtedly knew Dalrymple very well and he spent some weeks in 1772 at the village school. At that time it apparently stood on the site of what is now the White Horse Inn, previously known by the name St Valley. This same site became the original Free Church of Dalrymple in 1863. However, when the Church of Scotland and the Free Church were reunited in 1929, Dalrymple had two parish churches until 1936 when the former Free Church building closed and worship of the joint congregation began in the present parish church. The Free Church building had its roof removed and walls lowered and subsequently became the White Horse Inn. Today, anyone enjoying hospitality there may indeed feel the presence of the poet who was rather fond of Dalrymple. This important time at Dalrymple allowed Burns and his brother Gilbert to improve their handwriting and grammar and meet some other local lads. Because of the need to continue with work on the farm, Robert and Gilbert were sent to Dalrymple school week about. Before that Robert had acquired an elementary grounding in the 'three Rs' at Alloway (1765-67). In 1773 he spent an intensive three weeks with John Murdoch in Ayr improving his English and French and Murdoch introduced Burns to Latin. 1775 saw the poet studying mathematics among other subjects under Hugh Rodger, the Kirkoswald dominie.

Burns had several friends at the little hamlet of Purclewan, about two miles from Dalrymple. There he used to come to get his horses shoed by Henry McCandlish, the man who lent him *The Life of Wallace*, the reading of which aroused his life-long patriotism. The blacksmith's son, James McCandlish, who later dropped the "Mc" from his surname, studied medicine at Glasgow University and became a lecturer in medicine at Edinburgh, was an intimate friend of the poet, and one of his correspondents in later years.

In a letter of 1791 to Peter Hill, an Edinburgh bookseller, he describes Candlish as, *"the earliest friend except my only brother that I have on earth, and the worthiest fellows that ever any man called by the name of friend."* James married the "witty" Miss Smith, one of the famed Mauchline Belles. Dr Robert Smith Candlish, the celebrated leader of the Free Church, and Principal of the Free Church College, was their son. While he waited on the shoeing of his horses, Burns no doubt looked in to see Allan Kilpatrick, the miller, especially when there was a chance to have a word with the miller's daughter, Nelly, the "sweet sonsy lass" who charmed him on the harvest field at Mount Oliphant in 1773 when he was aged 14 and she was aged 12 or 13 years.

Nellie Kilpatrick later married William Bone, coachman at Newark Estate and she died about 1820. Perclewan Mill can still be seen today, but the hamlet has disappeared, and all that is left of McCandlish's smithy is an outhouse that forms part of the little farmstead.

Robert is also supposed to have attended dancing classes in a barn in Dalrymple, probably in 1775 when his family were still living at Mount Oliphant. Indeed some biographers go so far as to state that his friend, Nelly Kilpatrick, the subject of his earliest poem, Handsome Nell, was among the dancers who attended and in all circumstances this would hardly be surprising as entertainment of that nature would have been popular with young women allowed to attend by their parents. This seems to have been a secret adventure which the poet took great delight in and had to be careful to hide from his father who had a great dislike of such activities.

A picturesque bridge over the Doon at Skeldon.

O once I lov'd a bonny lass,
Ay, and I love her still!
And whilst that virtue warms my breast,
I'll love my handsome Nell.

My Handsome Nell
Robert Burns

Another, albeit slender link between Burns and Dalrymple, was that the cousin of the poet, William Burnes, was apprenticed to James Armour, a master mason and contractor who was responsible for building a number of bridges in Ayrshire. He also worked on Skeldon House, Dalrymple. Robert and his family were still living at Mount Oliphant when James Armour and his father-in-law Adam Smith built the Greenan Bridge over the River Doon on behalf of the Earl of Cassillis. Both masons names were recorded on the plaque on the bridge which was demolished in 1861 and replaced with the present bridge.

It seems that everywhere the Scots dialect is slowly dying out. Indeed the last statistical account observed this trait in the Parish of Dalrymple: *"Perhaps the greatest cultural shortcoming is that of speech. The old vernacular is almost extinct, and has been replaced by a debased and slovenly form of English."*

Dalrymple today is expanding, with private housing estates being built, but this is unlikely to change the quiet rural nature of the village. Newcomers do often bring a rich seam of ideas and energy and should be regarded as a positive benefit in any community. Change and stability are important elements for progress.

The bowling green is popular for older residents and the community centre, built on the site of the old school, has a regular programme of social activities for all ages. The local primary school caters for up to 160 pupils and was built in 1962 to replace the old school. There is an interesting war memorial of 1922 in Barbieston Road with an elegant octagonal cross, designed by James Miller and executed by William Vickers. The Kirkton Inn, built in early 1900 is a popular hotel and restaurant of note and it is complimented by the nearby Whitehorse Inn. Ayr is the focal point for social and recreational purposes. There is a good 'bus service from the village to the main town.

From Dalrymple the River Doon winds its way to the sea at Doonfoot, passing within a mile of the Auld Clay biggin, Alloway's Auld Haunted Kirk, the Burns Monument and gardens and the Burns Heritage Centre. It meanders under the famous Brig o' Doon where poor Maggie lost part of her tail in that vivid, inspirational epic poem, Tam o' Shanter. Visitors can hardly fail to think about Robert Burns in this Land o' Burns where his presence is palpable. Humanitarian, national icon, poet and musician, lover and internationalist. He is arguably Scotland's most remarkable and best-loved son. Nowhere captures his legacy more effectively and authentically that in Alloway, the poet's birthplace. Now a world-class museum and visitor centre where many folk over the years will doubtless have reflected on man's inhumanity to man and thought of Burns classic poem with its world-wide quoted verse appealing for common sense, understanding and perhaps above all, compassion.

For a' that an' a' that,
It's comin yet for a' that
That man to man the world o'er
Shall brithers be for a' that.

Above the banks of the river and near to the Brig of Doon is the hotel of the same name. Popular with visitors and locals alike, this excellent hotel with its inspiring backdrop of Burnsiana, hosts weddings on the famous Banks o' Doon. Like 'Halloween,' Tom o' Shanter draws heavily on the lore of witchcraft, which Burns learned so vividly from the stories of Betty Davidson, and is so evocative at Alloway as the River Doon flows gently and salutes the nearby Firth of Clyde. Our journey has now ended - enjoy the photographs

Now, wha this tale o truth shall read,
Ilk man, and mother's son, take heed:
Whene'er to drink you are inclin'd
Or cutty sarks rin in your mind,
Think! Ye may buy the joys o'er dear:
Remember Tom o' Shanter's mare.

Tam o' Shanter
Robert Burns

CHAPTER 15
A HISTORY IN PICTURES
A brief photographic record of the Doon Valley and its people

To make a happy fireside clime
To weans and wife,
That's the true pathos and sublime
Of human life

Epistle To Dr Blackstock
Robert Burns

Most of us relish looking at photographic scenes of people, places and events of yesteryear in communities special to us. They often evoke happy memories of bygone times when life perhaps seemed simpler and happier. Doon Valley folk who are now settled firth of these shores, seem to especially appreciate books of this sort. As all of us get older, there is a tendency to reflect on the days of our youth and remember the folk who touched our lives in special ways. Perhaps we did not always appreciate them in our youth, but as we speed forward in the journey of life, it can be revealing and humbling to reflect on our formative years. Enjoy these photographs. If they take you on a magical journey down memory lane, the author will be absolutely delighted!

Members of the Dalmellington Home Guard snapped at the town's War Memorial circa 1939. There were two shifts of Home Guard in Dalmellington and this would be one of the shifts. Most of the names are unknown, but a few have been identified.
5th from left front row: Tommy Hutchison; 6th Neil Dempsey; 9th Charlie Baird;
5th from right second front row: Adam 'Addie' Johnstone; 4th from right third row: George Orr (Butcher); 5th from right third row: Jimmy Hay: 9th from right 3rd row Sam Wilson; 2nd back row third ? Murphy.

PT Class with Mr Alex Scott at Dalmellington 1951.
Back row: John Carlisle, Robert Bell, David McMurdo, Tom McClymont, Jim Hamilton, David Connell and Billy Donnelly.
Front row: Jim McQuade, John Blackwood, Mr Alex Scott (PT teacher), Tom Hutchison, Duncan Torbet and Andy Park
On ground: Gordon Ireland, Billy Gillespie and unknown.

Bellsbank Primary School Class of 1958. Joseph Rhodes is currently head teacher at Dunoon Grammar School and being a former pupil, attended the 50th anniversary celebration of the opening of Bellsbank School on 24 June, 2005.
Back row (l to r): Billy Blain, Gordon Davidson, Joseph Rhodes, John Pollock, Stewart Walker and James Orr.
Middle row: Donald McDonald, George McCreath, Robert Dunn, Tom Bowie, ?, Sandy Murphy, Drew Clydesdale, Andrew Hannah, Billy Thomson, teacher Mrs Burton.
Front row: Alice Saunders, Agnes McCurdie, Jennifer Anderson, Mary Dunn, Betty Johnstone, Janet Hutchison, Jennifer Jess, Maureen Wilson, Moira McHendry and Mary O'Neil

Patna Badminton Club 1962 in the Church Hall.
Back row (l to r): ? Hastie, Hazel Black, Andy McCubbin, Tom White, Ian Blain, Walter McCubbin, Jim Grant, Jean Galloway and Alistair Johnstone.
Front row: Catherine Wallace, Rita Findlater, Jessie McHattie, Jean McCartney, Christine McClellend and Peggy Docherty.

This photograph was taken in 1904 or 1905. William May, who retired from the Secretaryship of The Dalmellington Iron Company Ltd, in January 1928, lived with his wife Jeanie (nee Boyle), and their children Neil Allan, Claude Simpson and Jeanie Boyle, at "Hillhead House", Waterside, and later at "Rathan", Carsphairn Road, Dalmellington. He is pictured here with his younger son, Claude, who served in the 17th. Service Battalion, Highland Light Infantry, and died at the Somme on 1st. July, 1916, aged 23; his name is on the War Memorial at Waterside. William May died on 7 May, 1930 and is buried in Ayr Cemetery.

Patna Public School in 1960. Back row (l to r): teacher ?, ?, ?, A Kirwood, J Stewart, J Pettigrew, A Currie, R Law, J Cran, D Brown, ? Ashley, B Robertson, Billy Boyle, J Goodwin and D Robertson. Second back row: Gordon Robertson (teacher), A Ballantyne, J Graham, ? Whiteford, ?, ?, A Lindsay, M Lafferty, A Graham, E Stevenson, ? Clark, J Smith, J McDougall, J Fitzsimmons, J Bradford, J Logan, M Finlay, H Lymburn and Mr May (teacher). 3rd back row: ? Graham, C McDonald, A Kennedy, M Knox, M Gillespie, M Torbet, J McWilliams, L Graham, I Johnstone, E Ferguson, E Dinwoodie, M McCallum, A Knox, A McDerment and teacher ? Second front row: S Lang, E Hamilton, M Tinman, E Thomson, M Murray, M Boyle, M Thomson, A Ballantyne, J Grant, J Kilpatrick, A Hainey, E Brown, J McGuigan and E Black. Front row: G Graham, J Lynn, T McBride, ?, J Bryce, K Ferguson, ?, ?, G Peters, J Faulds, ?, and J Graham.

Burnfoothill Primrose in the 1920s. The 'Hill, although relatively remote above the Doon Valley, had some excellent sporting, recreational and social activities. Back row: George Bowie, Adie Park, Tommy Anderson, Hugh Givens, ?, Buller Dalziel, James 'Pimpy' Moffat and James Graham. Front row: Sam Gillespie, David Logan, S Riddicks, James 'Ruchie' Leslie, Jimmy McDowall, Jim 'Elkie' Clark and Tommy Kirk. The young lad holding the shield is George Sturgeon who was later a miner. His son, George, still lives in Dalmellington.

Grave in the grounds of Craigengillan House of Lizette, a dog which died in 1934. There are six other marked graves of pet dogs in the grounds. The earliest grave dates to 1900.

A photograph of previous winners of the Cecil Oughton Memorial Slow Melody competition taken at the diamond jubilee event in Dalmellington Community Centre on April 9, 2005. The 2005 event was won by one of Scotland's top trombonists, Derick Kirkwood from Mauchline and educated at Auchinleck Academy.

Back row (l to r): David Roxburgh, Stephen Reid, Calum McPhail, Sandy McCulloch, Sandy Pollock, David Pratt and Derick Kirkwood.
Front row: John Boax, Jimmy Graham, Allison Bonnar, Eleanor Ferguson, Robert Dunn and Sandy McAughtrie. Some of these players are regarded as among the finest brass musicians in the UK. All are proud of their association with Dalmellington Band.

Dalmellington School class of 1933. Many are no longer with us whilst others are among the older citizens of Dalmellington. Many will instantly recognise well known Dalmellington folk of yesteryear.
Back row (l to r): G Stevenson, H Hose, W Riggens, J Brown, W Auld, J Hill, J Hewitson, P Johnston and J Bryan.
Second backrow: J Wilson, J Filson, B McKnight, M Murray, J Bowie, J Buchanan, J Wallace, M Waugh, M McInnes, M McClure, Jean Hill, A Anderson, M Gavin, M Thompson and B McLarty.
Second front row: M Clydesdale, J Blain, J Orr, L Keary, J Calderswood, M McTear, M Kirkland, R McKenzie, M McInnes, H Small, N Hainey, N McCutcheon, J Gemmel, J Brown, B Findlay and M Baird.
Front row: T Orr, J Keen, P McCutcheon, N Graham, W Steel, Bert McClue, J Pollan and Hugh Clark. Teacher: Miss M Morrison. Headmaster, Mr James Brown.

Athletics presentation of trophies in Dalmellington with Councillor Alex Johnstone on hand to do the honours. Many will immediately know many locals in this shot.

Dalmellington High School class of circa 1955 are a really happy lot!
Back row: John Buchanan, Jim Innes, John Douglas, Gordon Baxter, Roy Colquhon, Roy Wright, John Logan, Arthur Moffat and David Limond.
Second back row: Drew Orr, William Barnes, Tom Gray, Alex Bryson, Robert Neil, John Boyle, Robert Hill, Jim Bryce, David Hare and Scott McCall.
Front row: Grace Graham, Alice Ireland, Doris McNae, Diana Lee, Sandra Blain, Helen Hill, Evelyn Stevenson, Dorothy McLelland, Violet Taylor and Maureen Boyle
Seated: Robert Galloway, Marion Wallace and Alex Anderson.

Dalmellington Junior Secondary School sports day circa 1955. The 3rd year class were putting on a Highland Dance display. Front row (l to r): Corinth Ross, Hazel Boyd, Christine McClelland, Rachael Black, Jean Brown, Jean McHattie, Anita McLeod and Moira McLean.

The River Doon issuing from the loch as it would have been prior to the building of the Loch Doon dam in 1935. This photograph is very early 1900s.

Bellsbank Primary circa 1964
Back row (l to r): John Kirk, Jim Auld, John McGraw, Jim Cassels, Sam Wilson, ?, Andrew Givens, Jim McHattie, ?
Middle row: Mrs Elizabeth Logan, Dale Mellis, ?, Elizabeth Dempsey, Mary Kay, Ray Torbet, ?, Annette Uriarte, Christine McArthur and Mr Hector McDonald.
2nd front row: Jack Givens, ?, Jim Murphy, Margaret Kennedy, Susan Barber, Betty Steele, ?, Lawrie Coughtrie, ?, Francis Clark.
Front row: Danny Whiteman, Sandy Whiteside, Billy Cowan, Bobby Cameron, Tommy Hanns and Robert Copeland.

Dalmellington High School class of 1956/57
Back row (l to r): Jim McNae, John Boyd, Billy Douglas, ?, George Gourlay, Billy Shankland, McDonald, ?, Frances Kennedy and Blane,
Second back row: Jim McCabe, James Whiteford, Hugh Clark, John McWhirter Jimmy Torbet, John Burns, Andrew Currie, ?, Jim Scobie and Eric Irvine.
Second front row: Mary McPhail, Lizzie Scobie, Marlyn Steele, ?, ?, ?, ? and Anne Kennedy.
Front row: Wilma Barbour, Katherine Wallace, ?, May Black, ?, Claire Clellend, ?, Marion Stead, Anne Lindsay and Susan McCreath

Dalmellington Band bass section with bandmaster William Oughton, taken in the Band Hall around 1953. This group had just won the Ayrshire contest.This qualified them to go to the Scottish Championships where they played Eric Ball's Quartet for Tubas and took 4th prize.
Back row (l to r): Hugh Johnstone, later conductor of the band and lifelong servant who was awarded the MBE for his services to brass banding; Robert Oughton (conductor) and Willie Kennedy, another valuable and unsung servant to the band.
Front row: John Paulin and Jim Hose.

Bellsbank Primary School class of circa 1963.
Back row (l to r): Walter McNaught, Jim Ferguson, Billy Hamilton, Sandy McHendrie, Tommy Martin and Francis Goudie
Second back row: Mrs Young, Alex Kylnesky, Drew Murdoch, Billy McKinstry, John Robertson, David Dempsey, Adam Brown and Tommy Hillhouse.
Second front row: John Stevenson, Elizabeth Hainey, Jean Auld, Grace Bell, Donald Tyson, Anne Telfer, Francis Allan, Betty Inglis, Jim Connell.
Front row: Jean Maxwell, Nan Steele, Jean Ferguson, Nan Baird, Margaret Hainey, Christine Melnitschuk, Wilma O'Neil, Margaret Kellock, Christine Telfer.
Seated: Ucilla Johnstone, Helen Clark and Esther Strachan.

Bellsbank School concert circa 1960 with pupils of several classes gathered for a photograph.
Back row (l to r): Sheena Pollok, Ucilla Johnstone, Christine Telfer, Margaret McLay, Donald Tyson, John Robertson, John McGraw, Orr, Sandy McHendrie, ? and Sam Wilson
Second back row: Jean McMillan, Annette Uriarte, Esther Strachan, Mary Kennedy, Elizabeth Dempsey, Bobby Plain, Robert Copeland, Albert Whalen, Jack Givens, George Sturgeon, Joe Ferguson, ?, and ? Anderson.
Second front row: Ian Burns, ?, ?, Molly Grant, Isobel Whalen, Irene Finlay, Steven Rogers, Billy McDicken, ?, ?, ?, and ?
Front row: Nan Young, Caroline Jones, ?, Caroline Scott, (St Clements ?), ?, ? and Greer McHendrie.

3rd year class at Dalmellington High School in 1951.
Back row (l to r): David Jeffries, John Moore (local history author and former teacher), Bobby Bell (Dalmellington baker), Jim Baird (son of Patna Head Master of that period), Bobby McCreath, and Head Master Mr Thomson
Front row: John Ireland (haulage contractor in Dalmellington), George Allan, Jessie Wells, Cathy Reid (McLean), Grace Dyett, Bobby Wallace and Bertie Clydesdale.

Dalmellington United 1900. The only person identified is the captain (third from left front), William Johnstone, father of Hugh Johnstone MBE.

Immediate front is Hugh Johnstone of 59 Burnton with some pals on a 1938 visit to Bill Johnstone who had joined Manchester City Police in 1933. The three men played with Craigmark Burntonians.
(l to r): Robert Boyle, Bill Bigham, Sandy Candlish and well known Dalmellington man, Hugh Johnstone then young lad of 14 at the front.

Tom 'TP' Park outside his home in Dalton Avenue, Dalmellington. He was quite ill and he was delighted at the band visiting him and he took the opportunity of playing the big drum. His wife, Mammie is standing behind him. In earlier years 'TP' was the band drummer. His son Andy Park was a well known composer and arranger and radio and TV executive. Mrs Peggy Hodgson is seated. The young man standing at the front is Tom Farrell.

This snap was taken at the rear of 59 Burnton about 1935.
(l to r): Bobby Wilson, Kate Murdoch, Marion Murdoch, Willie Murphy, Agnes Falconer and Hugh Johnstone. The Folconers stayed at 61 and the Murdoch's at 60 Burnton.

LMS 2P 4-4-0 No 642 at Dalmellington Railway Station in 1932. The Ayr and Dalmellington Railway opened for goods on 15 May, 1856 and for passenger services on 7 August. It closed for passengers services on 6 April, 1964 one of many branch lines to close under the famous Beeching cuts.

Dalmellington High School football team of circa 1965
Back Row(L to R): Donald Tyson, David Marshall,George MacDonald, George O'Neil,Jim McLelland and Bert Stevenston
Front Row (L to R):Jim McHattie, Joe Donachie, John Sloan, George Galloway and Malcolm Cullen

Bellsbank School class of 1961
Back row (l to r): Tom Wilson, Iain Burns, Jim Uriarte, Tom Whiteside, Charles Hose, Jim Wallace, John Coughtrie and ?
Second back row: Mrs McDonald (teacher), Brian McNaught, Hugh Uriarte, Brian Murphy, David Kearey, Sandy Whalen, William Kirpatrick, ?, ? and ?
Third back row: Ann Beaston, Mary McMillan, Margaret Jordan, ?, Elizabeth Harkness, Jean McConnachie, Elizabeth Black and Morag Montgomery.
Second front row: Margaret Auld, Ann McCutcheon, Helen McMillan, May Kirk, Isabell Armour, Margaret Riggans, Anne-May Jones and Ann McCulloch.
Front row: Tom Murphy, Sophia Jess, Margaret McLean and Andrew McRoberts.

Dalmellington Red Star football team
Back Row (L to R): Drew Johnstone, Terry Murray, Jimmy Torbet, Roy Wright, Robert 'Rab' Douglas, David Gillespie.
Front Row (L to R) David Kirk, Ian Bigham, David Hair, Rab Miller, Jamsie Whiteford, James O'Neil.

Dalmellington High Grade School about 1930 with teacher, Granny Williamson.
Back row (l to r): Robert Clement, John Sharp, Arthur O'Neil, Willie Murdoch, Sydney Murray, Kemal McCartney, Matthew Johnstone and Robert Johnstone.
Second back row: Tom Calderwood, John McCracken, Willie McInnes, George Reid, John Calderwood, James Gilfinnan, Findlay Ross, Robert Kean, James Pettigrew and Charles Trafford.
Third back row: Barbara McKenzie, Elizabeth Melville, Agnes Calderwood, Catherine Sheddon, Peggy Mills, Molly Baird, Mary Rae and Agnes Brown
Second front row: Jean Greig, Mary Findlay, Nicholas McLarty, Elizabeth Yates, Nan Murdoch, Jessie Marr, Bella Young, Sadie Calderwood, Annie Buchanan, Chrissy Findlay and Peggy Steele.
Front row: Christine McVean, Rose Torbet, May McKee, Agnes Orr, Lexa Pyper, Bella Small, May Rodger and Margaret 'Tottie' Coughtrie.

Lethanhill School circa 1928. Perhaps older readers may be able to help identify others in this photo.
Back row (l to r): 5th along David Picken
Second back row: Rita Knox (Johnstone),
Front row: (last) Hugh Ferguson.

Rev Ninian Wright, outside the Kirk o' the Covenant Manse, located near to the Glebe and now part of a private housing development. This was in the early 1930s and he owned one of four or perhaps five cars in Dalmellington at that time. The other lucky car owners were Dr Howat, Mr Addison of Dunollie, and the proprietors of the Eglinton and Black Bull Hotels. If there was a car on the Moss Road when the train was on the line going into Dalmellington there was some excitement to find out which would reach the village first. Percy Hill's bus began a service to the valley in the 1930s, but most folk travelled to Ayr by the train. The sixpenny specials on a Saturday brought the shops, dancing at the Bobby Jones and cinemas within reach for villagers.

Dalmellington High School class of 1955.
Back row (l to r): Robertson, Torbet, Ian Boyle, John Graham, ?, Stewart McHattie, Billy Anderson, Fulton Muirhead and John Stark.
Middle row: William Boyle, Sylvia McLarty, Betty Rowan, Jean McHattie, Nancy Sutherland, Margaret Kerr, Marion Johnstone, Jean Brown, Pat O'Neil and Arthur Pettigrew.
Front row: Rachel Black, Christine McLelland, Annabel McDonald, Janice Allison, Agnes Currie, Hazel Boyd, Janet Donnelly, Agnes Thomson, Margaret Collins
Seated: ?, ?.

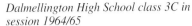

Dalmellington High School class 3C in session 1964/65
Back row (l to r): Jim Hyslop, George O'Neil, Fergus Grant, Billy Hamilton and Tom Gordon.
2nd back row: Tom Reid, Sandy Anderson, John Cowan, Peter Murray, Robert Sloan and James Caldwell.
2nd front row: Tom Farrell, Tom Jones, Colin Tulip, Sam Taylor, Henry Bell and Ian Stewart.
Front row: Joe Donachie, Arthur O'Neil, Tom Paulin, Bert Stevenson, Jim Clydesdale, Louis Uriarte and Alfie Jackson

Dalmellington Speedwells in 1960.
Back row (l to r): Mamie Johnstone, ?, ?, ?
Middle row: Nan Steele, ?, ?, ?, Betty Lamb, Irene Finlay, Kate Meechan.
Front row: Christine Melnitschuk, Jean Auld, ?, Kate McPhail, Jean Ferguson, Anne Armour and ?

Ye Old Castle House is a prominent building in Dalmellington's High Street. It was previously a public house with upstairs as a dwelling. The lady is Mrs Dora Carr. Her husband, Albert A Carr, from Silkstone, near Barnsley, came to Dalmellington where he was bandmaster of Dalmellington band from 1880 until 1909. Bob Thomson, a Fifer, took over that year as bandmaster. 1897 was the diamond jubilee of Queen Victoria and the band went to Carlisle and took part in a competition where they got 5th prize. The villagers were so elated that they bought Mr Carr an inscribed sword which can be seen in Cathcartson Museum. He was also put into Ye Old Castle House from his job in the local coal mines, so that he could concentrate on working with the band.

Dalmellington Army Cadet Force on an exercise in Camlarg Estate circa 1982 where they are examining the mysterious Spider stone, so called because of the concentric rings thereon. The leader is Willie Johnstone of Patna. All the cadets are from Dalmellington.

Primary 7 at Dalmellington about 1965. The class teacher was Miss Mary Hill, of whom one pupil recalled: 'A great teacher not only for school lessons but also taught us in a way that you never forgot. She emphasised what was right and wrong and all your good deeds added a brick to your house in heaven and bad ones removed two.'
Back row Boys: Stewart Mc Lean, George O'Neil, Willie McDowall, John Sloan, Tommy Reid .Tommy Gordon, Jim Johnstone, David Campbell and Robert Beatson.
2nd back row: Bert Stevenson, Charles 'Chuck' Baird, Robert Brands, Robert Brown, George Smith, Joseph Donachie,Jim Clydesdale, David Marshall, Jim Wilson.
2nd front row:Sadie Smilie of Burnton Farm, May Auld, Caroline Park, Jennifer Murdoch of Dalcairnie Farm, ?, Rona McHattie, Bridgett Price, Ellen Findlay, Grace Dempster.
Front row: Margaret Mc Whirter, Agnes Millar, Margaret McLean, Mary Easton, Faye McDicken, Janet Duncan .Annette Coughtrie, Linda Bunyan and Barbara Newlands.

A special railtour arrived along the Ayr - Dalmellington branch line allowing the enthusiasts to visit the Ayrshire Railway Preservation HQ at Minnivey just behind Burnton. This branch line closed to passengers in 1964

Lethanhill School football team in season 1958/59 which can be seen on the football. This was the second last 'Hill team. Mr Robert Taylor was the last headmaster, serving for a few months until the school closed in December 1959
Back Row (L to R): George Donohoe (headmaster), Richard Law, Billy 'Bunts' Hunter, David Brown, Andy Paterson, (Goalkeeper), George 'Punt' Ferguson, Willie Young, John McDonald and Matt McLelland (teacher)
Front Row: Tom Tusler, Boyd Plenderleith, Tommy 'Tucker' Campbell, Tom 'Max' Murray, Billy 'Buck' Robertson, Alex 'Shy' Kirwood and David Fossett. ?.

Staff at Lethanhill School circa 1952.
Back row (l to r): ?, ?, ?
Front row: Miss Parker, James Paterson, later headmaster Bellsbank Primary School, George Donohoe, headmaster and unknown. Even Mr Paterson could not recall the names of the females in this photograph. No doubt the minute this book is published everyone will know who they are!

Bellsbank Primary School circa 1959
Back row (l to r): Francie Clark, David Lees, John Kirk, Jim Murphy, Bobby Cameron, Jim Steele.
Middle row: Nan Carr, Anne Millar, Sheena Pollok, Danny Whiteman, Sheena Duncan, Jean Harkness, Margaret McCartney, Elizabeth Dempsey, Annette Uriarte, Robert Copeland, Hazel Duncan and Ray Torbet.
Front row: John Nixon, Donald Reid, Sam Wilson, Gordon Murdoch, Richard Paulin, Greer McKay and ?

Rev Kenneth Yorke with members of session and congregational board at Dalmellington Parish Church when James Lees Reid received a long service certificate as elder.

Dalmellington High School of circa 1963
Back row (l to r): Mr Irvine (headmaster), Clifford Wilson, Billy Blane, George Dunn, Hugh McCreath, William Donnan, Ian McDowall, John Riggins, David Stewart, Billy Coughtrie, William Reid and Billy Thomson
Middle row: Doris Jackson, Isobel Bryson, Ellen Logan, Jean Bell, Marlyn Rattray, Shona Limond, Anne Dempster, Carol Rae, Laura Rudland and Jennifer Anderson.
Front row: Joan Steele, Jean Grant, Janet Hutchison, Hannah Wallace, Eleanor Storrie, May Barclay, Jean Barbour, Ella Maxwell and Lillian Hewitson

Dalmellington High School class of 1959
Back row (l to r): Charles Kennedy, Andrew Logan, Campbell Johnstone (son of the Patna Minister).
Middle row:Robert Curtis, John Lawrie, John Blackwood, Andrew Burns, William Paterson (current butcher in Dalmellington), David Frame and William Kennedy (son of late John P Kennedy, headmaster of Bellsbank School 1955 – 1968)
Front row: Margaret Harvey, Margaret Ritchie, Agnes McBurnie, Christine McDonald (daughter of Rev McDonald of Lamloch Church), Jan Scott (Waterside), Ann Smith (Clawfin), Sheila Ballantyne, Madge McBurnie and Lyn Buchanan (now in Australia).

No doubt many readers will identify someone they know from this Dalmellington Primary School class.

A class at Lethanhill School 1947/48.
Back row (l to r): Andrew Meldrum, Andrew Beggs, Jean Meldrum, Margaret McFarlane, Lilly Gilmour, John McEwan and John Kennedy
Middle row: Billy Johnstone, Margaret Johnstone, Ella Knox, Marjory Fawcett, Elizabeth Dalziel, Helen Torbet and Bert Daly
Front row: John McDermont, Francey Bryce, Billy Brown, Harry Ferguson and Hugh Gilmour.

Awe-inspiring Dalcairney Falls in 1947 when there was a very severe winter. The boys are silhouetted against the gleaming wall of ice. They skipped Sunday School on learning of this magical frozen waterfall and were snapped as they stood on the ice. This photo never ceases to amaze the author.
(l to r): Hugh Hainey, George Auld, Robert Auld and Tom Leitch.

Whaup Row, Lethanhill looking towards Greenhill and the Loch Doon hills. The row was later rased to the ground and is now sadly covered in conifer trees like the rest of Lethanhill.

Dalmellington Rangers in 1921. Only the very oldest Dalmellington residents will recall some of these players.
Back row (l to r): Bob Hewitson, J Riggins and Joe Millar.
Middle row: B Dempsey, R Hill, H Cannon, J Findlay, T Stewart, A Orr and R Park.
Front row: B Blackwood, J Campbell, W Tyson, J Hainey and J Torbet.

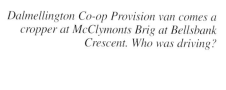

Dalmellington Co-op Provision van comes a cropper at McClymonts Brig at Bellsbank Crescent. Who was driving?

The year 2000 was very special and Bellsbank School decided to have the whole school photographed together. Can you spot someone you know?

Patna Amateurs in 1959-60 when they had a very good team and won four cups that season. Tommy Campbell died in Australia.
Back row (l to r): John Thomson, John Duncan, Duncan Robertson, John Pirrie (Ayr), George Ferguson, Tommy Walker, Willie Young and Andrew Beggs.
Front row: Andrew Patterson, Tommy Campbell, Alex Kirkood, Billy Campbell (Ayr), Billy Robertson, Andrew Black and Maxwell Murray.

4th Class of 1965 at Dalmellington High School.
Back row (l to r): Hugh Kerr, Adam Watson, David Seawright, David McLarty and Jack McLelland.
Middle row: Catherine McCulloch, Maureen Bolton, Nan Stevenson and Janice Ritchie.
Front row: Kathleen McPhail, Jeanette Coughtrie, Dougal McCall, Janice McCracken and Anne Reid.

Benbeoch Craig on 27 January, 2005. The open cast mining operations will eventually infill all the spoil from mining extraction.

Burnfoothill Primrose in season 1918-19 displaying several trophies.
Back row (l to r): W Bryden, R Park, R Campbell, W McClymont and Tommy Kirk.
Middle row: G Bryden, H Ferguson, R Murray, R Carlile, G Anderson, P Grant, T Ballantyne and H Davidson.
Front row: W Hood, T Knox, W Ballantyne, J Hainey, A Ballantyne and R Denham.

Six Dalmellington men on holiday in the Isle of Man in the 1930s.
Back row (l to r): Bert Wallace, David Wallace, Willie Paterson and Jim Wallace.
Front: William 'Wull' Currie and Alex Wallace.

Doon Harriers were the local athletic club based at Benwhat where this photo was taken in 1948. The club produced many fine athletes over the years.
Back row (l to r): William Currie, Walter McEwan, George Hannah, George McConnell, Neil Robertson and Addie Hannah.
Middle row: Jimmy Galloway, Jim Bigham, Robert Mullen, Richard Armour, George Mowat, Andrew Filson and Bruce Hainey.
Front row: Tommy Filson, Tom Wilson, John Wilson, Andrew Galloway and Eddie Uriarte.

Two local boys from Patna, Hugh Scobie and Douglas Peters, joined the Junior Leaders Regiment in 1977. Both were former pupils of Patna Primary and Dalmellington High School. During his training at Bovington, Hugh reached the rank of Junior Squadron Sergeant Major and finished his last term by winning the Inniskilling Cup. On passing out he was posted to the 13th/18th Royal Hassars in Germany. Douglas, who won the Royal Tank Regiment Bowl, another of the championship awards was a junior corporal and later passed out to join the 4th Royal Tank Regiment in Germany. Both lads were members of the Army Cadet Force in Patna before joining up. At the passing out parade the soldiers received their awards from the inspecting officer, Lt. General Sir Robert Ford, who as a recruit also trained at Bovington.

(l to r): Mr Tom Peter, Douglas Peters, Brian Peters, Mrs Betty Peters, Mr David Scobie, Iain Scobie, Hugh 'Fergus' Scobie, Mrs Jean Scobie

Dalmellington Hotspur Team 1945/46 which didn't last for too long, the players dispersing to other local teams.
Back row (l to r): Willie Biggam, Robert Boyle and Jock Johnstone.
Middle row: Willie Dempsey, Bob Burgess, Harry Kennedy, Billy Travers, John Scobie, Billy Campbell, Lewis McArthur and David Scobie.
Front row: Tommy Lafferty, John 'Jubie' McCulloch, Owen Murray, Jim McCracken and Tom Blackwood.

Long Live the Hill was the tribute erected in memory of this lost village of Lethanhill. All that remains today is the war memorial and ruins of houses within the large plantation of trees adjacent to the memorial.

*Underground at Pennyvenie Pit,
Dalmellington which closed in 1978.
(l to r):John Craig, Sam McLarty, George
Sturgeon and Hugh Rogers.*

*Pennyvenie Colliery with Burnton in the
background. Colliers Row can also be seen
on the left side of the road with the pithead
baths straight ahead on the opposite side.*

*Lethanhill School 1956. The village of
Lethanhill had been demolished by that time,
but the school remained open until 1969 with
the children bussed from Patna. Where are
they all now and what are their memories of
the 'Hill?*

EPILOGUE

Memory of happy days in the hills of Galloway, so close to my own heart, always bring a twinkle to the eye as I think of stunning scenery cycling over the Merrick; exploring the shores of Loch Enoch; visiting Backhill o' Bush or Tunskeen Bothy with wonderful companions - Peter Barr of Kilmarnock, Bill Frew of Sorn and the late Billy Piper of Prestwick. All larger-than-life characters, whose love and knowledge of the highways and byways of Ayrshire and Galloway was infectious. I recall many poignant visits to the remains of the Lost Villages of Doon Valley. Places such as Lethanhill, Benwhat, Corbie Craigs, Craigmark and Beoch. Thinking back to the residents, mainly hardy miners and their families, who inhabited these lonely villages is very touching and humbling.

Standing on the windswept moors at North Beoch and looking at the ruins of the once bustling row and the remains of the outdoor toilet block of the school, I think of my father, James Lees Reid, and his brothers and sisters who were raised at remote Beoch. His was a large family tryng to make ends meet in the 1930s, a difficult time for many working folk in the Doon Valley. My late mother, Mary Hose was reared at Craigmark, near Dalmellington, also of a large family. With many other women, including my aunt Margaret Hendry (Hose), she worked as a labourer in the woodyard at Dunaskin during the war years. Hard, back-breaking work. And yet she had happy memories of everyone getting stuck in and being proud to do a job to help the war effort.

All of us have the opportunity to reflect on family and friends who have touched our lives in special ways. I am extremely proud of my Doon Valley roots and the many folk who helped influence and shape my life. I think of people like Hugh Johnstone MBE and his total dedication to hundreds of young musicians in Dalmellington Band and local schools. His contribution to the Doon Valley and the world of brass banding has been truly remarkable. My own parents were determined that I would never work in the coal mines, so my chosen career took me to the Ayrshire Constabulary in 1967 and then Strathclyde Police, an enjoyable, challenging and enriching career.

In retirement I enjoy nothing better than taking my young grandson, Taylor, on my weekly visits to the Valley of Doon to visit my father, his great grandfather in Dalmellington. Loch Doon is visited almost every week, because it beckons and beckons as it has done since my boyhood days. I look forward to my grandson Taylor James Reid (18 months) reaching the stage when I can take him on longer walks and tell him about this fascinating corner of Ayrshire.
I enjoy reading the poems of Robert Burns, Robert W Service and W D Cocker and warmly commend them to the reader. Having the opportunity of

But pleasures are like poppies spread,
You seize the flow'r, its bloom is shed;
Or like the snow falls in the river,
A moment white - then melts for ever.

Tam o' Shanter
Robert Burns

A grateful, warm adieu;
I with a much indebted tear
Shall still remember you!

The Farewell
Robert Burns

writing about the Doon Valley has been enormously enjoyable.

On 24 June 2005 I had the pleasure and honour of attending the 50th anniversary celebrations of my first seat of learning, Bellsbank Primary School. The old school has only had four headmasters in that time. The first was John P Kennedy (1955 - 1968), the 'heidi' in my time. He was followed by Maxwell B Geddes (1969 - 1975), James Paterson (1976 - 1988) and Alexander Kennedy took up his post as head teacher on 16 August 1989. The school today is a vibrant, happy place with a lovely welcoming atmosphere. It was poignant to see the display of photographs reflecting 50 years of the school showing former pupils and teachers whom I remember with great affection. The concert put on by the children in the afternoon took me back to my own days treading the boards at Bellsbank School. The school roll has fallen from 450 down to under 200 because much of Bellsbank has been demolished in recent years. Also, young people have to leave the Doon Valley to find work elsewhere. However, the commitment of the teaching staff is still inspiring with the school being in good heart and now embarking on the road to its centenary. The words of the late Arthur Wilson can be adapted from the High School of Dalmellington to suit this great little primary school and hopefully the pupils of today will take this to heart.

May the sons of our sons remember,
Bellsbank School with pride

The children sang a birthday song of three short verses to celebrate this special milestone and they literally lifted the roof singing the final verse:

Happy birthday everyone,
Every teacher, child and friend,
Thanks for all your help and patience,
Happy birthday, Bellsbank School.

Finally, there is a quiet satisfaction in knowing that my Doon Valley books will hopefully be read by folk who follow in my footsteps, perhaps 100 years hence. That, I find intriguing and somewhat satisfying.

FURTHER READING

The Statistical Account of Scotland, Vol. 6, Ayrshire, 1791-1799

Robert Hetrick, *Poems and Songs,* 1826

George S Hendrie, *The Parish of Dalmellington,* 1889

John Paterson, pamphlet entitled: *Reminiscences of Dalmellington,* 1902

Charles Dougall, *The Burns Country,* 1904

George Colville, *Dalmellington Manuscript,* 1926

Hugh Gibson, *Woodrow's Manuscript relating to the Covenanters who fell in Dalmellington Parish 1666 – 1668* (Reprinted 1928)

Matthew Anderson, *Poetical Works of Matthew Anderson,* 1928

Wilson MacArthur,*The River Doon,* 1952

David L Smith, *The Dalmellington Iron Company: its Engines and Men,* 1967

Hugh Douglas, *Portrait of the Burns Country,* 1968

John Moore (ed), *Gently Flows the Doon,* 1972

John Moore (ed), *Among Thy Green Braes,* 1977

Robert Farrell, *Benwhat and Corbie Craigs,* 1983

Peter Connon, *An Aeronautical History of the Cumbria, Dumfries and Galloway Region Part II (1915 – 1930),* 1984

George Hill, *Tunnel and Dam,* 1984

Andrew Boyle, *The Ayrshire Book of Burns-Lore,* 1985

T Courtney McQuillan, *The 'Hill – Its People and its Pits,* 1988

James Mackay, *Burns – A Biography of Robert B*urns, 1992

Rob Close, *Ayrshire & Arran,* 1992

Donald L Reid, *Old Dalmellington, Patna & Waterside,* 2001

Donald L Reid, *Doon Valley Memories, Dalmellington, Dunaskin, Patna & District, A Pictorial Reflection,* 2002

Dane Love, *Ayrshire: Discovering a County,* 2003

Richard Dargie, *Scottish Castles and Fortifications,* 2004

Donald L Reid, *Doon Valley Bygones,* 2004

Donald L Reid, *Yesterday's Patna & The Lost Villages of Doon Valley,* 2005

The following books have been written by Donald L Reid.
* *Reflections of Beith and District – On The Wings of Time,* 1994
* *Yesterday's Beith – A Pictorial Guide,* 1998
The Beith Supplement – The Story of Beith's Newspaper, 2000
+ *Old Beith* (Stenlake Publications) 2001
In The Valley of Garnock – Beith, Dalry & Kilbirnie, 2001.
+ *Old Dalmellington, Patna & Waterside,* (Stenlake Publications), 2001.
* *Doon Valley Memories, A Pictorial Reflection,* 2002
Beith Bygones – A Pictorial Journey Down Memory Lane, 2003

Readers may, like the author, find extremely helpful information in the following books and articles, some of which may be available in the reference section of East Ayrshire Library Headquarters, Kilmarnock and at the Baird Institute, Cumnock Library. *Old Dalmellington, Patna & Waterside* is published by and available from Stenlake Publishing, The Square, Catrine, Ayrshire KA5 6RD.

Barrmill Jolly Beggars Burns Club – Reflections On A Diamond Jubilee, 2003
* Doon Valley Bygones, 2004
* Yesterday's Patna & The Lost Villages of Doon Valley, 2005

* Book no longer in print
+ Book available from Stenlake Publishing, 54 – 58 Mill Square, Catrine, KA5 6RD

FORTHCOMING BOOK
Donald L Reid's next book, *Ayrshire's Doon Valley – Through the Lens*, will be published in May 2006

Donald is always keen to obtain more photographs of people, places and events relating to the Doon Valley. All photographs will be scanned and immediately returned. It is also important that a brief resume is given of the photograph including names and the approximate date. The contact address is:
Donald L Reid, 7 Manuel Avenue, Beith, Ayrshire KA15 1BJ Tel: 01505-503801 or E: donaldleesreid@hotmail.com

DALMELLINGTON BAND – KEEP THE MUSIC FLOWING
Dalmellington Band is based in the small village of Dalmellington in the South West of Scotland, 60 miles south of Glasgow. It is one of Scotland's oldest Brass Bands and has been in the forefront of the movement since its formation in 1864. The band have had notable success in contests and have their name inscribed on every major competition trophy in Scotland, including 3 Scottish Championship wins.
They have recently achieved the long-term aim of delivering a state-of-the-art band hall, which was a major and commendable achievement.

For many folk Dalmellington is synonymous with its brass band with its proud reputation for friendliness and excellent team working. If you wish to be associated with ensuring the long-term future of the band you may wish to consider becoming a patron or making a donation. Visit the band web site at:
www.dalmellingtonband.org.uk or contact them by e-mail:
contactus@dalmellingtonband.org.uk.

For further information about the patron scheme contact band president Bert Ritchie, 'Glenauchen.' 10 Ayr Road, Dalmellington, Ayrshire KA6 7SJ. Telephone 01292-550250.

"May the sons of our sons remember, Dalmellington with Pride."

AUTHOR PROFILE

Donald Reid was born and brought up in Dalmellington where he attended the local High School. He has lived in Beith for the past 20 years. His childhood ambition was achieved when he joined the Ayrshire Constabulary as a Police Cadet in 1967. When he retired in 1999 he had been a Police Superintendent for 7 years as sub-divisional officer with responsibility for operational policing in Glasgow City Centre. Donald is married to Kathleen and his son Fraser and daughter Elaine are both holders of the bronze, silver and gold Duke of Edinburgh awards. Elaine has also achieved her Queen's Guide Award. His pride and joy is his grandson, Taylor who was born in March 2004 and he has the great honour of looking after him on three days each week - a joyous privilege.

Donald has twice been president of Barrmill Jolly Beggars' Burns Club and is their secretary. A regular on the after dinner speaking circuit, particularly at Burns Suppers, Donald has spoken at events from Invernesshire to Staffordshire.

A keen enthusiast of the works of the Preston born poet, Robert W Service, whose formative years were spent in Kilwinning, Donald and his good friend Iain D Shaw FSA Scot regularly speak to groups and organisations on the life and times of the poet in an illustrated lecture entitled, Robert W Service - Poet of the People. In 2002 Donald proposed the toast to Robert W Service at the Kilwinning Branch of the Robert Service Commemorative Society's third annual dinner. He is also a past chairman of Garnock Valley Round Table. Over the last 18 years most of Donald's spare time has been taken up in his voluntary role as leader of Beith Open Award Group. This was one of the largest Award Groups in Scotland and he is particularly proud that 46 young people have obtained the prestigious gold award with the group over the last 8 years.

A past president of Garnock Valley Round Table, Donald was accorded the honour of Beith Citizen of the Year in 1994 for his voluntary work in the local community, but as his pal, Iain Shaw, constantly reminds him, "Beith's not that big a place." He is a member of Beith and District Community Council and co-ordinated their bids for the Calor Scottish Community of the Year in 2003 and 2004 when Beith were finalists and received honours in several categories including old people, young people, community life and community business. He is an occasional driver for Garnock Valley Disability Group. He is the Ardrossan & Saltcoats Herald's prolific local correspondent for Beith and district, keeping readers up to date with happenings in the town and district.

In 2002 he founded and is secretary of the Dr Henry Faulds - Beith Commemorative Society which successfully raised funds and established

DONALD L REID BA FSA Scot, *author, who was written several other local history books on the Doon Valley.*

I am taking the old road again,
By the dyke-side, down to the green glen;
And the breezes in the rowans red,
Whispers in trees of my childhood,
"Come you this way again."

The Old Road
Maureen Henderson

Blessings on the old road again,
By the dyke-side, down to the green glen;
And the beauty of rowans red,
And the carefree days of my childhood,
Which will not come again.

The Old Road
Maureen Henderson

a fitting international memorial in his home town to the Beith born pioneer of fingerprint science. He is a director of the Radio City Association, which delivered a Healthy Living Centre to the Garnock Valley. He is a member of Beith Civic Week working group with the 2005 event the largest for several years.

In earlier days, Donald played trombone with Dalmellington Band and Dunaskin Doon Band. He has been a guest dress and deportment adjudicator at the West of Scotland Band Championships and the prestigious Land of Burns Competitions for several years. An ardent local historian whose main interest in the Garnock and Doon Valleys of Ayrshire, in earlier days was a very keen hill walker and cyclist whose great love was the ever-beckoning hills of Galloway. He enjoys looking back on happy days awheel with Billy Frew (Sorn) and Peter Barr of Kilmarnock, albeit a back injury prevents him cycling now. Donald's philosophy is simply to live life to the full every day.

How Daur ye ca' me "Howlet-face"
Ye blear-e'ed, withered spectre?
You only spied the keekin glass,
An there ye saw your picture.

The Keekin Glass
Robert Burns